HOMELAND SECURITY
OPERATIONAL ANALYSIS CENTER

Supporting Threat Reporting to Strengthen School Safety

Findings from the Literature and
Interviews with Stakeholders
Across the K–12 School Community

PAULINE MOORE, JENNIFER T. LESCHITZ, BRIAN A. JACKSON, CATHERINE
H. AUGUSTINE, ANDREA PHILLIPS, ELIZABETH D. STEINER

This research was published in 2022.

Approved for public release; distribution is unlimited.

About This Report

The U.S. Department of Homeland Security's (DHS's) Cybersecurity and Infrastructure Security Agency (CISA), in collaboration with the U.S. Secret Service's National Threat Assessment Center (NTAC), asked the Homeland Security Operational Analysis Center (HSOAC) to provide enhanced tools for kindergarten through 12th grade (K–12) schools and school systems to improve school safety. As part of this task, HSOAC analysts drafted a series of reports on the basis of comprehensive literature reviews on school safety and security and interviews with stakeholders from the K–12 school community. This report draws on existing literature on threat reporting and leverages knowledge gained from a series of interviews with state-, district-, and school-level stakeholders from across the country to identify best practices for encouraging students to report threats. In addition to CISA, NTAC, and DHS more broadly, the primary audiences for this research are school- and district-level administrators and school safety personnel. State, local, tribal, and territorial government and law enforcement personnel, as well as school-related associations and stakeholder groups, might also be interested in this research.

This research was sponsored by CISA's Infrastructure Security Division's School Safety Task Force and conducted within the Infrastructure, Immigration, and Security Operations Program of the HSOAC federally funded research and development center (FFRDC).

About the Homeland Security Operational Analysis Center

The Homeland Security Act of 2002 (Section 305 of Public Law 107-296, as codified at 6 U.S.C. § 185) authorizes the Secretary of Homeland Security, acting through the Under Secretary for Science and Technology, to establish one or more FFRDCs to provide independent analysis of homeland security issues. The RAND Corporation operates HSOAC as an FFRDC for DHS under contract HSHQDC-16-D-00007.

The HSOAC FFRDC provides the government with independent and objective analyses and advice in core areas important to the department in support of policy development, decisionmaking, alternative approaches, and new ideas on issues of significance. The HSOAC FFRDC also works with and supports other federal, state, local, tribal, and public- and private-sector organizations that make up the homeland security enterprise. The HSOAC FFRDC's research is undertaken by mutual consent with DHS and is organized as a set of discrete tasks. This report presents the results of research and analysis conducted under task order 70RCSA20FR0000056, K–12 School Security Doctrine Development.

The results presented in this report do not necessarily reflect official DHS opinion or policy.

For more information on HSOAC, see www.rand.org/hsoac. For more information on this publication, see www.rand.org/t/RRA1077-3.

Acknowledgments

We would like to acknowledge the numerous stakeholders across the K–12 school community for their participation in interviews and for offering candid insights into approaches to threat reporting in their schools, districts, and states. Their willingness to share their experiences and provide input into our study greatly improved our work. We thank our sponsors from CISA and NTAC, whose support and feedback were indispensable in creating a research product that we hope will benefit local education agencies and other stakeholders across the United States. We would also like to acknowledge and thank our reviewers, Bob Harrison and Heather L. Schwartz from the RAND Corporation, whose feedback enhanced the value of this report.

Summary

Despite the consensus that exists around the importance of violence prevention efforts in kindergarten through 12th grade (K–12) schools, existing research has revealed little about how to promote reporting among people who become aware of possible threats so that action can be taken. Notably, we believe that the effectiveness of different approaches to reporting is likely to vary considerably across different school contexts.

This report helps fill this gap by illuminating the variety of threat reporting models available to K–12 schools across the country, as well as the approaches school leaders can use to support individual decisions to report threats in a way that will work best for their school environments. The report is part of a larger effort by the Cybersecurity and Infrastructure Security Agency's School Safety Task Force to provide enhanced tools for K–12 schools and school systems to improve school safety through the development of a tool kit on threat reporting in K–12 schools, as well as the published *K–12 School Security Guide* (CISA, 2022), "School Security Assessment Tool (SSAT)" (CISA, undated), and associated K–12 school physical security training companions.

This study drew on a review of the literature focused on threat reporting and threat reporting systems, with particular attention to how their design and structure, as well as student- and school-level factors, can affect student willingness to report potential threats. It also drew on more than 30 interviews conducted with stakeholders across the K–12 school community in the United States intended to identify current approaches to encourage reporting, strategies for success, and the challenges that schools and districts face in this area. Interviews with stakeholders at the state, district, and individual school levels provided insight into a varied set of reporting models in place across the country at the level of states, school districts, counties, and local communities.

The audience for this report includes a variety of stakeholders. In addition to informing the development of a threat reporting tool kit for K–12 schools published by the Cybersecurity and Infrastructure Security Agency in collaboration with the U.S. Secret Service's National Threat Assessment Center, it is also our intent to make this report accessible to local education agencies and individual schools across the United States. The report can also be of value to grant-making institutions and elected legislators who enact laws in support of school safety. We highlight seven main implications for school safety planning from our research:

- **Strong relationships between students and school staff are essential to building trust and robust reporting cultures.** Trusting school climates in which students feel comfortable going to an adult with their concerns are the foundation of productive approaches to reporting. Local education agencies can enhance trust between students and school staff by increasing opportunities for teachers and staff to interact informally with groups of students outside the classroom (for example, during school sporting events, theater and musical performances, or other gatherings) and ensuring that school police, school resource officers, and other security personnel receive training to help them work and communicate effectively with school staff, administration, students, parents, and the broader school community.

- **Approaches to reporting are likelier to support all members of the reporting community, including students, if they emphasize accessibility and cater to common ways in which today's student population communicates.** Schools and districts should work to make numerous avenues available to students and other community members who want to come forward with information. Formal programs set up to promote reporting—such as tip lines—should be widely accessible to students and the broader reporting community (via, for example, mobile device applications).

- **An anonymous reporting option can help address student fears of being ostracized by their peers as a result of reporting.** Anonymous reporting systems allow people to submit tips without providing any information that can be used to identify them. Although anonymity poses some complications in following up on tips, stakeholders in the K–12 community across the United States agree that the benefits far outweigh the costs. Hosts of anonymous reporting systems should clearly message to their communities whether and under what specific conditions people's anonymity could be forfeited. Alternatively, schools and districts can host confidential reporting systems, in which information about the person reporting is collected but kept private.

- **Reporting programs that give students and others the option to speak or chat directly with an operator trained to interact with people in crisis provide additional support to youths and can lower barriers to reporting for those not comfortable speaking directly with law enforcement.** Many state- and district-level tip lines across the country make trained operators available to people reporting, in part to avoid perceptions that reporting programs are tied to law enforcement. Trained operators, such as crisis counselors, can also provide immediate support to people reporting suicidal ideation or self-harm. Schools and districts should consider their unique contexts to decide who should be responsible for fielding reports coming in through tip lines and whether they will require law enforcement support to field and triage tips (for example, in the case of tip lines available 24/7 to the reporting community).

- **Building awareness and implementing training on the importance of reporting and the means through which students can report information are critical to supporting people seeking to come forward.** Students are likelier to report when they are aware of the means at their disposal and know when and what to report. Regular training and outreach—for example, every two years—can help build this knowledge. There is value to tailoring training materials to make them relevant to specific school contexts and more resonant to many student bodies (via, for example, scenarios and vignettes related to reporting). Engaging students themselves in training and outreach can also help lower barriers to reporting among their more-reluctant peers.

- **Transparency in and communication about how schools act on information reported through a tip line or via other methods influence students' willingness to come for-**

ward. Annual and other periodic reports to the reporting community can increase transparency around critical issues, such as when information is shared with law enforcement and when situations are left exclusively to school administrators. Ideally, information contained in a program's annual reports would help support both the program's legitimacy and its efficacy.

- **Gaining buy-in from school leadership, teachers, and other school staff increases the chances that a reporting program will be effective and sustainable.** School leaders and staff are critical to a reporting program's success. However, the introduction of new responsibilities related to reporting places additional burdens on staff. When implementing a new program, local education agencies can ease this burden by offering clear guidance and training around staff roles in the reporting process and providing staff with teaching material to increase students' knowledge about reporting.

Contents

Figure and Tables

Figure

Tables

CHAPTER ONE

Introduction

Behavioral threat assessment (TA) programs in kindergarten through 12th grade (K–12) schools and the associated teams of school and other personnel responsible for these programs are designed to identify and respond to a situation in which someone could pose a threat to a school community. The nature and content of what are considered "threats" can vary widely, including threats or ideations of carrying out targeted attacks, engaging in self-harm, and committing various criminal and drug-related offenses. To friends, family, and other parties who seek intervention assistance for someone they consider at risk of mobilizing toward violence, TA programs provide alternatives to automatically involving law enforcement or criminal prosecution (Center for Prevention Programs and Partnerships, 2021). Early detection and intervention are important not just to protect the public but also to respond to a situation in which someone is at risk of turning to violence and acting to redirect that person before they move too far down a path that will adversely affect their lives and those of others (Cornell, 2020).

Ultimately, the prevention of school-based violence depends on schools, public safety organizations, and others becoming aware of the potential threat that someone poses. In fact, in a U.S. Secret Service (USSS) study of completed attacks, researchers found that, in 81 percent of school shootings, at least one person knew that the would-be attacker was planning a violent event (Vossekuil et al., 2004). In a more recent study of 67 averted plots to attack schools, researchers found that almost all would-be attackers (94 percent) shared their intent to carry out an attack, either said to someone or through electronic messages or posts online (National Threat Assessment Center [NTAC], 2021). Nearly 70 percent of these would-be attackers shared their intent with their peers.

However, past studies of targeted violence incidents also show that, even in cases in which people observed warning signs of potential violent behavior in others, they did not consistently report those signs to law enforcement or other parties (Craun et al., 2020). Individual willingness to report possible incidents represents a fundamental constraint on communities' ability to prevent school violence: Even an ideal intervention program cannot successfully respond to potential violence if they do not become aware of the risk until it is too late.

A variety of factors might explain low levels of reporting: Some people might question or be unaware of the importance or significance of the behavior they observed, or they might have a different interpretation of events. Others might be concerned about the consequences for the potential attacker involved, fear social recrimination, or lack trust in the organizations to which they could report (e.g., law enforcement). Indeed, a study of 15 people with prior knowledge of potentially deadly school attacks showed that people who shared information about a planned attack had positive connections to either school officials or the school itself; those who did not share clues in advance had no connection to the school or believed that school staff would not react positively to their doing so (Pollack, Modzeleski, and Rooney, 2008). Studies of averted school shootings also show that students report threats to different adults: Students go primarily to school administrators, teachers, and school resource officers (SROs) but are less likely to contact non–school-affiliated law enforcement directly (Stallings and Hall, 2019). A USSS study also revealed that school staff were most often the recipients of information about potential plots, followed by law enforcement, SROs, mental health providers, and other adults (NTAC, 2021).[1] These findings highlight the importance of establishing clear lines of communication and reporting procedures between students and their academic communities. They also have significant preventive implications, demonstrating the importance of creating threat reporting and TA teams that include a multidisciplinary set of people from the school community whom students, parents, and community members trust enough that they will be willing to report potential threats of violence.

Although there is agreement about the importance of violence prevention efforts in K–12 schools, we know less about how to implement models that support people who seek to come forward with information. Schools across the country have adopted different approaches to encourage reporting, often based on their local contexts; options include technological models focused on tip lines and personnel-focused models that center on building relationships between students and school staff. Other reporting models might be more interdisciplinary in nature and involve a variety of personnel who work to create trusted spaces for people to report potential threats, such as teachers, school psychologists, social workers, or school law enforcement. In areas where there are strong relationships among students, local communities, and law enforcement, having police as the primary point of contact might be preferred. However, in cases in which those relationships are weak or damaged, having other entities in the lead (e.g., counseling or medical organizations, social service agencies) could be more effective. On the whole, it is unclear which models are likelier to be effective in certain contexts than other models, and it is unlikely that a single "recipe" could work well in all areas or school systems.

---

[1] In a USSS study of 67 averted plots of targeted violence against schools, researchers found that school staff were the recipients of initial reports about plots in 28 cases (42 percent of the total). Law enforcement received initial reports in 20 cases (30 percent), SROs received initial reports in eight cases (12 percent), and mental health professionals received initial reports in two cases (3 percent). Other adults, such as parents, received initial reports in seven cases (10 percent) (NTAC, 2021).

Purpose and Approach

This report helps to better define the variety of threat reporting models available, as well as the context-specific approaches school leaders can use to encourage people's decisions to report threats in a way that will work best for their school environments. The report is part of a larger effort by the Cybersecurity and Infrastructure Security Agency's School Safety Task Force to provide enhanced tools for K–12 schools and school systems to improve school safety, through the development of a tool kit on threat reporting, as well as the published *K–12 School Security Guide* (CISA, 2022), "School Security Assessment Tool (SSAT)" (CISA, undated), and associated K–12 school physical security training companions. The comprehensive set of tools is designed to assist local education agencies (LEAs) in building safe and secure learning environments that attend to the teaching and learning needs of various school communities.

The study reported here had a two-pronged approach:

- In the first phase, we conducted a review of the literature focused on threat reporting and threat reporting systems, with particular attention to how their design and structure, as well as student- and school-level factors, can affect student willingness to report threats.
- In the second phase, we conducted interviews with more than 30 state-, school district–, and local community-level stakeholders involved in TA and threat reporting across the K–12 school community to identify current approaches to implementation, strategies for success, and the challenges that schools and districts face in this area. Our interviews speak to various reporting models in place at the level of U.S. states, individual school districts, counties, and local communities. We also strove to ensure that our selection of examples represented variation along such factors as specificity to the K–12 school community (i.e., we included school-specific reporting systems and reporting systems used by the broader community), geographical region and setting, composition of TA teams responding to reports, involvement of law enforcement in receiving and responding to reports, and reporting mechanisms and mechanics. We provide more detail about our interview process and analytical strategy later in this report.

The audience for this report includes a variety of stakeholders. As noted previously, the report will inform the development of a threat reporting tool kit for K–12 schools published by CISA. It is also our intent to make this report accessible to LEAs and individual schools across the United States; a central purpose is to help school and district leaders better implement effective and inclusive threat reporting systems that will contribute to making schools safer. The report can also be of value to grant-making institutions and elected legislators who enact laws in support of school safety.

Organization of This Report

The rest of this report consists of three chapters and an appendix:

- Chapter Two provides a review of the literature on school threat reporting systems and willingness to report threats and misbehaviors in the context of academic environments.
- In Chapter Three, we describe our interview selection and analysis methods and provide an overview of different approaches to threat reporting in place at school districts across the United States. This chapter focuses on describing the various strategies that schools, districts, and states employ to build trust with the reporting community and strengthen reporting, as well as the challenges that they have faced in doing so.
- Chapter Four summarizes our main findings and outlines implications for stakeholders in the K–12 school community.
- An appendix reproduces our interview protocol.

CHAPTER TWO

Review of the Literature

The literature on threat reporting in K–12 schools shows that a variety of factors influence student willingness to report threats, including bullying, weapons in school, and plans for violence.[1] In addition to individual factors, such as student age and demographics, such factors as school climate, the processes schools initiate and follow up with after they receive threat reports (e.g., the extent to which reports remain anonymous, or the actions that follow receipt of a tip, such as TAs), and students' knowledge of these processes and trust in personnel responding to reports all affect students' willingness to report concerning behaviors (Harrington, 2002; Hollister et al., 2014; Stohlman and Cornell, 2019; Stueve et al., 2006; Sulkowski, 2011; Syvertsen, Flanagan, and Stout, 2009; Wylie et al., 2010). As a result, joint guidance from the U.S. Department of Education and the USSS stipulates that schools can benefit from "ensuring that they have a fair, thoughtful, and effective system to respond to whatever information students bring forward" (Fein et al., 2004, p. 19).

In this chapter, we first describe the approach we took in our review, then continue with a discussion of the individual factors and features of school environments that are important to consider as schools seek to support people who want to come forward with information about threats and other concerning behavior. The chapter follows with a description of various features of school threat reporting systems and associated processes and procedures and a discussion of how these features influence willingness to report.

Literature Review Approach

The findings in this section are based on an exploratory review of the literature on threat reporting conducted between October 2021 and January 2022. To identify relevant sources, we conducted internet searches to capture existing federal, state, local, and nongovernmental guidance on reporting. The purpose of this search was not to conduct a comprehensive review of the reporting systems that exist at these levels but rather to identify a represen-

---

[1] In the TA process as it applies to K–12 schools, *threat* is defined as "an expression of intent to physically or sexually harm someone. This expression may be spoken, written, or gestured. Threats can be expressed directly or indirectly to the victim or others, and threats may be explicit or implied" (see National Association of School Psychologists, 2015).

tative set of strategies in place across the country that facilitate reporting across the K–12 school community. We draw on programs, policies, and guidance in place across some of these states, to the extent that they provide detail on processes and procedures that could affect student willingness to report.[2]

We also conducted searches of the academic literature focused on threat reporting, both within and outside the K–12 school environment. To date, most of the literature on threat reporting in K–12 schools has been nested in research about broader TA processes (i.e., what is done after a threat has been reported) and the extent to which various TA models contribute to successful outcomes in the areas of student well-being, perceptions of safety, and violence prevention. The majority of studies we reviewed addressed reporting in the context of this broader process; a smaller number of studies were limited to addressing just threat reporting and issues involving willingness to report. Of note is that we did not identify any studies that involved assessing the effectiveness of various approaches to reporting, including anonymous tip lines. As of this writing, any studies included in our review that directly addressed tip lines were largely descriptive in nature.

Finally, we searched for and reviewed relevant literature from sectors that face challenges comparable to those encountered in the K–12 school environment in reporting threats or concerning behavior. The goal in broadening our review was to take advantage of work addressing similar problems in other contexts, such as suicide, sexual assault, domestic violence, and violent extremist activity. These other realms of harm and violence prevention face the same challenge that schools do in ensuring that students know when and how to report threats and trust the reporting process. As noted with respect to the literature on threat reporting in the K–12 school environment, the literature that we identified on threat reporting from other sectors does not focus on assessing the effectiveness of various programs and is largely limited to understanding factors related to people's willingness to report.

We performed searches using Google and Google Scholar and reviewed references from highly relevant papers to identify sources for inclusion in our review. Our search terms included the following:

- *school tip line*
- *school threat reporting*
- [state name] *anonymous school tip line*
- *threat reporting school violence prevention*
- *willingness to report*
- *student willingness to report.*

---

[2] Maintaining and operating a school safety tip line is not a federal requirement in the United States, per the Every Student Succeeds Act (Pub. L. 114-95, 2015) or other legislation. Nevertheless, many states have implemented tip lines, and some mandate their use by public school districts in the state. Existing state-level tip lines are managed and operated by various state-level government agencies, such as offices of attorney generals, departments of public safety, and departments of education.

The sources we reviewed include federal, state, and local school district guidance; peer-reviewed and other published literature and research; and policy- and issue-specific briefs. We did not limit our search to specific publication dates, given the small number of relevant hits returned by our searches, and the emerging nature of research focused specifically on threat reporting in the K–12 school environment (and more broadly across other sectors).

Factors Influencing Reporting

Student- and school-specific factors play an important role in influencing students' willingness to report concerning behaviors. Most of these factors relate to characteristics of the student body (such as demographics) and characteristics of the broader school environment (such as levels of trust and perceptions of feeling safe at school, as well as communication and transparency around school safety procedures). Although some of these factors are not related to threat reporting systems specifically, they are an essential part of the discussion insofar as they have the potential to affect how schools design, implement, and promote threat reporting programs to make them effective.

Student-Level Factors Affecting Reporting

The literature shows that such factors as student gender, race and ethnicity, age, and performance in school, as well as individual attitudes toward reporting and the extent to which students feel safe at school, all influence willingness to report (Crichlow-Ball and Cornell, 2021; Hollister et al., 2014; Nekvasil and Cornell, 2012). A consistent finding is that older students, male students, and students of color are often less willing to report threats than younger, female, and white students (Aiello, 2019; Crichlow-Ball and Cornell, 2021; Hollister et al., 2014; Stohlman and Cornell, 2019; Unnever and Cornell, 2004; Wylie et al., 2010). The finding that students of color are less willing than white students to report concerning behavior might be corollary to the finding that U.S. schools with greater proportions of students of color tend to use more-punitive control measures to address disciplinary issues, such as law enforcement and security personnel, than schools with lower rates of racial and ethnic minority enrollment do (Irwin, Davidson, and Hall-Sanchez, 2013; A. Payne and Welch, 2015). According to existing research, these measures generate distrust among students of color about how school authorities will treat their peers and therefore also decrease propensities to report concerning behavior (Slocum, Esbensen, and Taylor, 2017). In addition to harboring feelings of distrust, studies also show, students of color are less likely than their white peers to seek help for bullying and threats of violence because they have different attitudes about how to deal with bullying (Eliot et al., 2010). Research also shows that students who perform well in school and achieve high grades are more willing to report concerning behavior than students who perform less well or who engage in delinquent activities (Connell, Barbieri, and Gonzalez, 2015; Hollister et al., 2014; Wylie et al., 2010).

Indeed, trusting relationships between students and school staff are critical to encouraging reporting (Fein et al., 2004; Yablon, 2010; Yablon, 2020). In a joint USSS and U.S. Department of Education study, researchers found that people who reported information about perceived threats did so in part because of trusting relationships they had with at least one adult, such as a teacher or other school staff member (Pollack, Modzeleski, and Rooney, 2008). These reporters also believed that school staff would take their information seriously and act on that information (Pollack, Modzeleski, and Rooney, 2008). Hollister and his coauthors found that students were likelier to report threats when they harbored positive feelings toward specific aspects of a school safety system, such as campus police or school administrators (Hollister et al., 2014). Unnever and Cornell also found that middle schoolers who perceived teachers to be unresponsive to bullying concerns were less willing to report their concerns than students who believed that their teachers would take action (Unnever and Cornell, 2004). Schools in which students have strong relationships with teachers and perceive their teachers as able to help them have higher reporting rates (Eliot et al., 2010); these positive relationships accrue through repeated student–teacher interactions, familiarity between students and teachers, and teachers making themselves accessible to students (Yablon, 2010).

School-Level Factors Affecting Reporting

Factors associated with the broader school environment can also correlate to school community members' willingness to report. A 2021 USSS report on averted targeted violence plots against schools, for instance, stresses "the importance of schools establishing and maintaining a safe school climate where students are empowered to speak up if they see a friend or classmate in distress" (NTAC, 2021, p. 21). Relevant factors that lead to higher levels of reporting include students having positive perceptions of school (Syvertsen, Flanagan, and Stout, 2009) and strong student connections to the school community and the availability of support systems (NTAC, 2021; Pollack, Modzeleski, and Rooney, 2008; Sulkowski, 2011). For example, studies have shown that students are less likely to report in schools characterized by cultural norms supportive of "street code," in which reporting is perceived as "snitching" and students fear retaliation if they report their peers' bad behavior (Slocum, Esbensen, and Taylor, 2017). Lindsey Wylie and her colleagues also found that schools with stronger collective identities and reduced levels of conflict were likelier to demonstrate willingness to report across their student bodies (Wylie et al., 2010).[3] Slocum, Esbensen, and Taylor further showed that students who were more "committed" to their schools were also more willing to report peer misbehavior, such as cheating, bullying, and theft, than students who felt weaker

---

[3] Notably, Wylie and her colleagues showed that, when a reporting program guarantees anonymity, the statistical significance of school climate in explaining willingness to report disappears (Wylie et al., 2010). This shows that particular characteristics of reporting systems are, in fact, important in influencing willingness to report, even in contexts in which levels of reporting might otherwise remain low (because of school or environmental factors).

connections to their school communities were (Slocum, Esbensen, and Taylor, 2017).[4] This is likely because students who feel more connected to their schools might also believe that victim services are more readily available, demonstrate trust in the school system, and perceive their school as adhering to a more "democratic authority structure" (Slocum, Esbensen, and Taylor, 2017, p. 127).

Perceptions of threats, as well as awareness of what should be reported and of the resources available to students, are also important factors that influence reporting. Steven Benjamin Schostak, for instance, found that K–12 students were likeliest to report threats that they believed were high risk and posed an imminent danger: They were likely to perceive direct, spoken threats of targeted school violence as higher risk than less specific threats and thus were more prone to report these types of incidents than other types of threats (Schostak, 2009). By contrast, students are less likely to take action in response to situations that they do not consider immediately dangerous and unlikely to cause severe harm. Moreover, in a study of the willingness of K–12 students to report peers carrying weapons at school, Connell, Barbieri, and Gonzalez found that students who were more aware of security measures in place at their schools—such as staff supervising hallways, locked doors, sign-in for visitors, locker checks, identification badge requirements, security cameras, and student codes of conduct—were likelier to report misbehavior than students who were not aware of any security measures (Connell, Barbieri, and Gonzalez, 2015).[5] Studies also show that college-age students who are less willing to report threats are generally less aware of campus resources (Hodges et al., 2016). Schools with robust victim and safety services "send the message that school officials are concerned about victimization" and therefore likelier to take reports of misbehavior seriously and act on them (Slocum, Esbensen, and Taylor, 2017, p. 142).

Indeed, the extent to which a school inform its community—particularly students—about the outcomes of reporting information affects willingness to report insofar as more knowledge about the downstream effects of reporting can increase people's propensity to come forward with information about concerning behavior. This dynamic can apply both at the *individual level* (feedback that demonstrates to someone who made a report that action was taken in their specific case) and at the *community level* (public reporting about what happens across all report cases providing objective information on the types of actions taken and the net effect on the student population).

Research shows, for instance, that procedural justice and public perceptions that police treat people fairly is an important predictor of victims' likelihood to report crime (Murphy and Barkworth, 2014; Socia et al., 2021). Similarly, perceptions of police effectiveness are driv-

---

[4] According to Slocum, Esbensen, and Taylor, 2017, students who were more committed to their schools than to negative peers or street code worked harder academically and were more driven to achieve success in school.

[5] However, other studies show that college students who feel safe at their institution actually demonstrate a lower willingness to inform authorities about concerning behavior; these students might be likelier than others to minimize problematic behavior or exonerate certain misbehaviors (Hollister et al., 2014).

ers of victims' or third-party observers' willingness to report (Rengifo, Slocum, and Chillar, 2019). If people believe that actions taken in response to criminal behavior will not be beneficial (or that the cost or risk of reporting to police will be larger than the benefit of doing so), willingness to report will weaken. Similar dynamics can exist in school community contexts, in which student and community assessment of the fairness and effectiveness of actions taken as a result of a report—and concerns about the consequences of reporting—could shape individual decisions to report.

In the K–12 school context, studies show that fear of specific outcomes resulting from reporting directly affect willingness to report: Students are more reluctant to report concerns when they expect a negative response from their teachers or from their schools more generally (see, e.g., Syvertsen, Flanagan, and Stout, 2009) or when they fear that police involvement will unnecessarily escalate certain situations (Hodges et al., 2016; Pollack, Modzeleski, and Rooney, 2008). Yet Pollack, Modzeleski, and Rooney highlighted that school policies do not always outline details about the school's role once information is received through a tip line or mechanism (Pollack, Modzeleski, and Rooney, 2008). These procedural details, however, are important insofar as they can help build the credibility of reporting programs and demonstrate schools' accountability and ability to follow through on reports. Negative assumptions about what happens after someone makes a report can also shape broader community views of threat reporting and TA efforts (i.e., beliefs that programs unnecessarily criminalize youth behavior and result in strengthening a school-to-prison pipeline). These dynamics could undermine willingness to report in individual instances of concern or result in broader opposition to threat reporting and TA efforts.

Options for Threat Reporting and Associated Processes

A wide variety of approaches to threat reporting and to promoting threat reporting exist in K–12 schools in the United States. Programs can support either anonymous or confidential reporting, and a growing number of states and districts are making multiple platforms available to their reporting communities while also encouraging informal approaches to reporting in schools, such as going to a trusted adult with information.[6] In addition, schools take different approaches to triaging and forwarding information about threats and include various personnel in the TA process that often follows the receipt of information. Some states require that threat reporting programs forward information to specific school or community stakeholders, such as law enforcement personnel, whereas others leave the decision up to individual school districts. Many districts, as well as some states, have developed robust training and outreach programs to promote threat reporting and make annual and other sta-

---

[6] A school's reporting community includes students as well as teachers and school staff, students' parents and other family members, and others from the surrounding community.

tistics available to the reporting community in an effort to build credibility and demonstrate accountability.

To address the finding that most students who carry out school shootings informed at least one other person about their intentions and desires (see, e.g., Meloy and O'Toole, 2011; NTAC, 2018; S. Payne and Elliott, 2011), many K–12 schools have placed renewed emphasis on the importance of instilling a "see something, say something" culture in their environments (Gorman, 2016). Efforts to promote reporting include informal approaches to reporting, such as encouraging students to go to a trusted adult with information about concerning behavior, and more-formal approaches that rely on established school safety tip lines, which create a structured system that students, school staff, parents, and members of the broader community can use to report concerns anonymously (Planty, Banks, Lindquist, et al., 2020). In today's environment, students and other members of the K–12 school community can report threats via numerous formats, whether spoken, via written notes and referrals, or through phone- or web-based tip lines (Cornell and Maeng, 2020; Planty, Banks, Lindquist, et al., 2020; Stein-Seroussi et al., 2021).

Tip lines receive significant attention as a school safety strategy (Blad, 2018; Planty, Banks, Lindquist, et al., 2020). They are intended to provide a channel for people to report potential threats and other concerning behavior, including instances of bullying and cyberbullying, self-harm, and drug use.[7] The variety of platforms available to provide information via tip lines (e.g., web, mobile applications, phone, text) also increases accessibility for users. In a 2019 review of state legislation, researchers found that 20 states required the use of tip lines in schools, and federal agencies have offered funding support to develop school tip lines (Planty, Banks, Lindquist, et al., 2020). In one survey of approximately 1,200 middle and high schools across the United States, about half (51 percent) reported having tip lines during the 2018–2019 school year; roughly 60 percent of these schools had implemented their tip lines within the prior three years (Planty, Cutbush, et al., 2021).

Anonymity and Accessibility

Fear of retaliation or being labeled a snitch is a significant barrier to reporting among the K–12 student population. As a result, many reporting platforms offer the option of anonymous or confidential reporting, ensuring that someone's identity will not be revealed if they choose to come forward with information. However, many anonymous tip lines also specify that anonymity can be forfeited under certain conditions: in the event of an imminent threat of violence (e.g., active suicide) or when someone submits a malicious false report (Planty,

---

[7] In fact, state-level school safety tip lines often receive more tips about concerns unrelated to school violence than they do about instances of school violence and can contribute to identifying other critical issues, such as the need to improve student mental health. In 2022, for example, Pennsylvania's Office of Attorney General released a report showing that "72.9% of the more than 80,000 Safe2Say comments have focused on instances of bullying, suicide and self harm, mental illness, or discrimination and harassment" (Office of Attorney General, 2022, p. 1).

Banks, Cutbush, et al., 2018). As an example, Nevada notifies its SafeVoice users that reports remain anonymous unless policies require disclosure of someone's identity in the case of a life-threatening situation or if the tip line is used unlawfully (Stein-Seroussi et al., 2021).[8]

Although offering options for anonymous reporting is widely promoted in the literature (Amman et al., 2017; Colorado School Safety Resource Center [CSSRC], 2020; Harrington, 2002; Hodges et al., 2016; Kelly, 2018; Kenny, 2010; NTAC, 2018; Wylie et al., 2010), anonymity has the potential to limit response effectiveness. For example, if someone provides only incomplete information, those fielding a tip might be unable to identify a student of concern and follow up appropriately (Fein et al., 2004; Stein-Seroussi et al., 2021). As a result, certain reporting platforms have been designed to include features to solicit specific information from reporters. For instance, web and mobile application platforms can include text fields in which a user can specify key details about a potential incident, such as the name of a school, the type of incident being reported, time and date of the potential incident, and the number of and physical characteristics of people involved (Stein-Seroussi et al., 2021). These fields simulate live prompting by an operator responding to reports provided via phone tip lines.

Moreover, school safety tip lines that make mobile applications and web platforms available to the reporting community are particularly effective thanks to their enhanced accessibility and edit features that allow users to update initial reports with additional information (Stein-Seroussi et al., 2021). Nevada's SafeVoice system makes a phone tip line, mobile application, and web browser with live chat options available to reporters in an effort to reach a broad user base and help gather as much information as possible. Colorado's Safe2Tell state reporting system offers similar features (S. Payne and Elliott, 2011), as do some state-level tip lines, such as Maryland's Safe Schools Maryland and Pennsylvania's Safe2Say Something.

Fielding Reports

Processes for fielding threat reports and the extent to which law enforcement personnel are involved in the school threat reporting process vary significantly across and within U.S. states. In its guidance, the USSS recommends that schools set clear thresholds for times and situations in which law enforcement is asked to respond to tips or take part in subsequent TAs (NTAC, 2018). Although reports of threats involving the use of weapons, threats of violence, or concerns about someone's imminent safety should be reported to law enforcement, issues involving bullying, drugs, self-harm, or depression most often do not require law enforcement involvement and are best left to school personnel (NTAC, 2018). Moreover, some state-level tip lines specify how they will handle prank tips and whether law enforcement will

---

[8] Policies on whether and how various school safety tip lines can access reporting individuals' phone numbers and internet protocol (IP) addresses vary by program. Many such policies are in place specifically to deter false or prank tips. In some states, for example, a reporting person's IP address is sent directly to law enforcement if the threat is deemed a life-safety event. Other states delete IP addresses from their systems after a set period of time, while others, to allow reporters true anonymity, do not track IP addresses at all (communication with USSS NTAC personnel, May 2022).

be involved in any related investigations, given that these contribute to increased workload and can threaten a program's sustainability. Pennsylvania's Safe2Say Something program, for instance, specifies that it can "trace false submissions only if a school gets a court order to uncover anonymity of a tipster" (Safe2Say Something, undated). Safe2Tell in Colorado also specifies that it "is required to protect the anonymity of reporters unless it is determined that a false report has been made through Safe2Tell with the intent to hurt, harass, or bully someone else" (Safe2Tell, undated a).

Various threat reporting programs across the United States have adopted different approaches to fielding reports from their school communities and to triaging information that comes into tip lines. In Florida, for instance, all school-related reports submitted through the statewide threat reporting program FortifyFL are automatically routed to designated school officials, as well as to local law enforcement; state law enforcement officials also have access to all tips submitted through this platform (FortifyFL, undated).

In Colorado, Safe2Tell was originally established in 2004 as a statewide anonymous reporting tool available 24 hours a day and operated as a public–private partnership combining safety resources of the Colorado State Patrol, the state's Department of Public Safety and Department of Law, and an independent board of directors (Safe2Tell, undated b). In 2019, the operation of Safe2Tell shifted to the Colorado Information Analysis Center, which staffs seven full-time analysts to respond to tips; these analysts relay all tip information to both local school and local law enforcement teams and follow up to verify that tips have been received and viewed in a timely manner (Colorado Attorney General, 2019).

Nevada's Department of Public Safety employs trained communication specialists to operate SafeVoice; these operators assign a priority level (critical, high, medium, or low) to each report the tip line receives, then triage reports to the affected schools and to relevant public safety agencies as appropriate (Stein-Seroussi et al., 2021). Specifically, every school administrator and each member of a school's SafeVoice team receives reports involving that school (regardless of priority level). Local law enforcement agencies receive only reports rated as critical (immediate threat of violence, self-harm, harm, or criminal acts directed at members of a school community) or high priority (potential for harm is high but not imminent or already concluded) (Stein-Seroussi et al., 2021).

In Nebraska, the state's pilot school safety tip line program, Safe2Help, is operated by a local nonprofit organization, Boys Town. Crisis counselors at Boys Town operate the tip line—available 24 hours a day, seven days per week—and determine, through communication with the reporter, what type of help is needed. The counselor then works with parents to create a plan that will ensure that the child receives support, and the counselor shares information with school officials, who follow up with the student. Local law enforcement is called to respond to reports only as a last resort—if, for instance, counselors are not able to communicate directly with parents or guardians or a report indicates that there is "an imminent danger" (Seaman, 2020).

Finally, it is important to note that someone reporting information through a tip line might not speak English. As such, many state-level tip lines, such as Safe2Tell in Colorado,

SafeOregon, and Safe2Say Something in Pennsylvania, make multilingual reporting forms available online or via their mobile applications.

Acting on Information

At the national level, the federal interagency clearinghouse on school safety, SchoolSafety.gov, emphasizes the importance of continuous threat report monitoring and follow-up as part of an effective approach to school violence prevention (see, e.g., Carlton, 2021). The TA process is an important part of the response and follow-up processes after information comes in through a threat reporting program.[9]

Current TA guidance for schools outlines several best practices related to following up on tips, including frequent monitoring, efficient management and processing of reports, responsiveness, and preparedness to act on reports (Cornell, 2011; CSSRC, 2020; Hollister et al., 2014; NTAC, 2018; Planty, Banks, Lindquist, et al., 2020). In its guidance to K–12 schools on preventing targeted violence, the USSS stresses the importance of establishing a multidisciplinary behavioral TA team (multidisciplinary team, or MDT) that will "direct, manage, and document the threat assessment process" (NTAC, 2018, p. 3). The USSS recommends that senior administrators at the school or district level lead these teams (NTAC, 2018). Behavioral TAs in schools are intended to prevent violence through the careful investigation of a particular situation and the subsequent design of an intervention strategy. Adapted from the USSS TA model, these assessments involve determining whether a student poses a threat and has the means to carry out a plan (National Association of School Psychologists, 2015; NTAC, 2018). Typically, the TA is initiated by reports of someone's concerning communications or behavior (Cornell, 2010).

Once information about concerning behavior is reported to a school, a designated team proceeds to gather information from the person of interest and from others, with the goal of determining whether or not the subject is demonstrating propensities for violence. In 2013, Virginia became the first state to mandate student TA across its public schools; by 2017, as many as half the secondary schools in the United States and more than 40 percent of primary schools used TA teams (Cornell, Maeng, et al., 2018; Meckler and Natanson, 2021).

School TA teams can be school- or district-based (i.e., a team responding to reports from multiple schools). For example, whereas superintendents in Maryland can determine whether TA teams should serve one or multiple schools (Maryland Center for School Safety, 2018), the state of Virginia mandates that each individual school have its own TA team (Virginia Center for School and Campus Safety, 2020). The composition of such teams also varies across states and school districts, depending on local legislation and mandates. Typically, school TA teams

---

[9] Some states require law enforcement participation in threat reporting (see previous section, "Fielding Reports") or that students receive training on threat reporting. Moreover, jurisdictions that require law enforcement participation in the threat reporting process do not always require that law enforcement then participate in the TA process. In general, NTAC guidance suggests that school personnel are best suited to lead the behavioral TA process (NTAC, 2018).

that respond to threat reports include education administrators, school counselors, mental health and social service providers, teachers, and sworn law enforcement officers (Center for Prevention Programs and Partnerships, 2021; Hansen and Diliberti, 2018). In Virginia, schools are required to put in place TA teams that include people with "expertise in counseling, instruction, school administration, and law enforcement," even if members fulfilling these roles are not currently serving in such positions at the school (Virginia Center for School and Campus Safety, 2020).

Some jurisdictions in other U.S. states have similar requirements or guidance on the composition of school TA teams (e.g., Maryland Center for School Safety, 2018; Office of Safe Schools, 2020; Ryan-Arredondo et al., 2001; Woitaszewski et al., 2018). The state of Nevada, for instance, mandates that public schools establish three-person teams to respond to information obtained through the state's SafeVoice threat reporting system and that each team include a school administrator and a school counselor, psychologist, social worker, or similar person if these are employed on a full-time basis (Stein-Seroussi et al., 2021). Notably, the involvement of law enforcement personnel on school TA teams also varies significantly. Some teams include law enforcement personnel employed directly by a school district and personnel employed by local law enforcement but assigned directly to a school or school district, such as SROs. Other districts and individual schools that have neither their own police forces nor SROs engage municipal or county law enforcement personnel.

School TA teams typically receive training on their responsibilities as they pertain to triaging and responding to tips about threats. Approaches to training vary by state, with some adopting train-the-trainer models for districts to train school staff and others requiring state-led training (Goodrum, Thompson, et al., 2018; Maryland Center for School Safety, 2018; Office of Safe Schools, 2020; Stein-Seroussi et al., 2021; Virginia Center for School and Campus Safety, 2020; Woitaszewski et al., 2018). Experts conducting recent evaluations of TA processes have recommended that educators apply a continuous improvement approach to TA procedures and to processes used to follow up on threat reports more generally (Cornell and Maeng, 2020; Goodrum, Thompson, et al., 2018). Some states are already doing this: In Virginia, for example, every member of a school TA team must complete state-level school TA training, including refresher training at least every three years and continuing education on related topics (Virginia Center for School and Campus Safety, 2020).

Communicating Outcomes

Many threat reporting programs used in K–12 schools include procedures for reporting outcomes and other information to the reporting community as a way of building the credibility of reporting systems and demonstrating accountability and follow-through. For example, Nevada's SafeVoice annual reports include a list of trainings provided to schools; these reports are available in the state's legislative research library. Pennsylvania's Safe2Say Something's annual report for the 2020–2021 school year included information on the changes made to training to account for remote learning during the coronavirus disease 2019 (COVID-19) pandemic. New options included self-guided training for students and virtual training for online classrooms. Colorado's Safe2Tell program releases annual statistics as required by statute and provides the following information:

- a summary of outcomes and actions taken on submitted tips
- the number of received tips, by category
- the total number of misuse incidents
- the number of tips involving a single incident
- the number of times someone used Safe2Tell to make a threat against someone else
- the number of times a reporting party was in crisis and reported to the program to receive assistance, and the time it took to identify the reporting party and respond
- the effectiveness of the Safe2Tell Watch Center
- recommendations for improving the program, based on available data (Colorado Attorney General, 2019).

Notably, tracking the outcome of situations reported through tip line programs and gathering data to compile annual and other reports distributed to the reporting community can be a time-consuming process. Moreover, certain stakeholders involved in the reporting process might be restricted in the amount of information they can provide about reporting outcomes because doing so could compromise open criminal investigations.

Providing Guidance and Outreach to the Reporting Community

To help them adequately respond to information they receive, some LEAs in the United States provide schoolteachers, administrators, and other staff with training on implementing reporting programs (Pollack, Modzeleski, and Rooney, 2008). Some recommended training topics include building knowledge and awareness of reporting programs through student and family orientation or new-student programs or integrating awareness efforts into existing initiatives that address related behaviors, such as bullying (Cornell and Maeng, 2020; Hodges et al., 2016; Stohlman and Cornell, 2019). At the level of U.S. states, some policies in place, such as those in Colorado, Nevada, Maryland, and Virginia, reference the importance of providing various types of guidance about reporting procedures to the reporting community. Colorado's Safe2Tell, for example, offers training to a diverse set of stakeholders across the reporting community, including students and school staff; many of these trainings are based on real-life scenarios. Safe2Tell also includes training programs designed specifically for school leaders and staff on how to share information, as well as materials aimed at guiding classroom discussion around the importance of reporting. Additional materials for other audiences are also available by request (Safe2Tell, undated c). Nevada's Department of Education developed training materials for districts to train school staff on reporting, and the state's Department of Public Safety provides training materials to law enforcement (Stein-Seroussi et al., 2021). Virginia's policy notes that school TA teams should provide their reporting communities with guidance on recognizing behaviors of concern and suggests integrating threat reporting programs with existing policies and procedures that address related issues, such as bullying, mental health, and substance abuse (Virginia Center for School and Campus Safety, 2020). Maryland's guidance provides similar recommendations, emphasizing that TA teams should provide instruction and training to their communities on recognizing concerning behavior (Maryland Center for School Safety, 2018).

Table 2.1 provides an overview of key features and trends from threat reporting tip lines currently in place in three U.S. states where such information was publicly available. The next section discusses ways in which many of the processes associated with threat reporting support building willingness to report across the K–12 student population.

How Reporting Processes Influence People's Willingness to Report

Despite the growth of reporting approaches as a way of responding to and preventing violence within the K–12 school environment, implementing a successful reporting system remains challenging. This section provides an overview of system features and practices as they affect trust-building and help encourage people to report—or dissuade them from reporting—threats.

Methods of Reporting Information

Generally speaking, the ability to anonymously report information about concerning behavior or other types of threats is viewed as an important feature to encourage reporting (Amman et al., 2017; CSSRC, 2020; Harrington, 2002; Hodges et al., 2016; Kelly, 2018; Kenny, 2010; NTAC, 2018; Wylie et al., 2010). For example, in a study of intervention strategies to prevent workplace violence, James Kenny found that anonymous surveys could increase employee comfort in reporting events to management and thus potentially help identify situations of concern (Kenny, 2010). Studies investigating the importance of anonymity in encouraging students in K–12 schools to report threats produced similar findings: Anonymous reporting platforms are significantly likelier to encourage reporting than approaches without anonymity as an option are (Stone and Isaacs, 2002; Wylie et al., 2010).[10] In cases in which maintaining anonymity is not possible, assurances that a reporter's identity will remain confidential can support people's willingness to report various threats, including in the K–12 school environment (Planty, Banks, Cutbush, et al., 2018; Reeves and Brock, 2018; Stone and Isaacs, 2002).

Additionally, data from existing state-level tip lines, as well as recent reports on the prevalence of tip lines across U.S. schools, suggest that making a variety of platforms accessi-

---

[10] Very little research exists on the outcomes of various reporting programs, including how they might affect willingness to report. For a review of ongoing research in this area, see Carlton, 2021.

TABLE 2.1

Features of Representative Examples of State-Level Tip Lines

State	Program	Tips Received				Most Common Event Type	Tip Line Operator	Tip Dissemination
		2019–2020 School Year	By Reporting Platform, as a Percentage					
			Phone	Mobile	Web			
Colo.	Safe2Tell	20,822	30	52	18	• Suicide threats • Drugs • Bullying • School complaint • Threats	Colorado Information Analysis Center–trained analysts	School administration; local law enforcement
Md.	Safe Schools Maryland	439	28	23	49	• Assault • Bullying • School complaint • Drugs • School attack	Maryland Emergency Management Association–trained analysts	District or school administration; 911 dispatch for emergencies
Pa.	Safe2Say Something	23,745	3	79	18	• Bullying • Suicide • Self-harm • Drugs • Smoking	Pennsylvania Office of Attorney General–trained analysts	District or school administration; 911 dispatch for life-safety tips

SOURCE: Colorado Attorney General, 2020; Maryland Center for School Safety, 2020; Office of Attorney General, 2021.

NOTE: All reporting systems represented in this table are anonymous tip lines. Event types are listed in descending order of frequency. For example, Colorado's most common event type is suicide threat.

ble to the reporting community works to encourage reporting (see e.g., Colorado Attorney General, 2020; Maryland Center for School Safety, 2020; Office of Attorney General, 2021; Planty, Banks, Lindquist, et al., 2020). Tip lines that make mobile applications available to their reporting communities might be especially valuable in supporting students who seek to report, given that they cater to a common way that today's K–12 student population communicates. Data from Safe2Tell in Colorado and Safe2Say Something in Pennsylvania show that the overwhelming number of tips for the 2019–2020 school year were received via mobile devices (Colorado Attorney General, 2020; Office of Attorney General, 2021), not via phone or web-based applications.

Guidance and Training on Reporting

Ensuring that the reporting community is aware of the importance of reporting, as well as of any systems and programs established to receive information, can also encourage people to come forward with information (Eliot et al., 2010; Haner et al., 2021; Pollack, Modzeleski, and Rooney, 2008). Training and outreach in the reporting community are especially important in this regard. In our review, we found that a variety of policies across U.S. states and individual school districts underscore the importance of communication with the reporting community and of building awareness of reporting programs. Specifically, training can reduce uncertainty about what and how to report and can contribute to increasing people's ability to recognize concerning behaviors (Haner et al., 2021; Henckel, 2019; Hollister et al., 2014; Stohlman and Cornell, 2019; Stueve et al., 2006).

Indeed, studies included in our review show that willingness to report various behaviors successfully increases when schools and other entities provide clear guidance to students, families, school staff (e.g., teachers, administrators, bus drivers), and other community members on what behaviors or activities should be reported, as well as guidance on how to identify such behaviors (Schostak, 2009). Familiarizing members of the school community with recognizable risk factors and warning signs has also increased people's ability to report threats (Bolante and Dykeman, 2017; Fein et al., 2004; Okada, 2015; Reeves and Brock, 2018; NTAC, 2018; Stohlman and Cornell, 2019).

Misunderstandings about privacy requirements can also negatively affect how schools act on reports, which can influence people's willingness to report in some school contexts. In a study of TA implementation with a student of concern who later committed a fatal school shooting, Sarah Goodrum and her colleagues found that school staff confusion about privacy laws reduced staff willingness to provide information about the student, including to campus law enforcement (Goodrum, Thompson, et al., 2018). Had staff been more aware of the safety exception under the Family Educational Rights and Privacy Act, they would have been likelier to share their concerns about that student.

In short, research on threat reporting in the K–12 school environment suggests that training school staff on the legal implications of reporting to school staff, as well as training tip line operators and TA teams on federal and state confidentiality laws, nondisclosure agreements, and privacy protocols to address a reporting person's concerns, can improve reporting (Goodrum, Thompson, et al., 2018; Planty, Banks, Cutbush, et al., 2018). Notably, increasing the entire school community's awareness of the importance of reporting—including messaging around how to identify concerning behavior, when to report it, and how to report it—is especially important when it comes to increasing willingness to report.

Membership of the Threat Assessment Team

Knowledge of follow-up actions taken once a school, law enforcement partner, or other partner has received information provided through a tip line or other reporting mechanism is critical to encourage reporting. It therefore follows that details of a school's TA process, including who is part of the team conducting the assessment, is an important factor to consider as schools seek to build trust and increase student willingness to report.

Many K–12 schools across the United States use MDTs to assess and intervene in response to specific situations involving students, as recommended by NTAC (NTAC, 2018). MDTs are a means of organizing and coordinating behavioral, mental, and physical health care services to meet the needs of specific individuals. For example, much of the literature on MDTs focuses on the use of such teams in medical and clinical settings (Doyle, 2008; Johansson, Eklund, and Gosman-Hedström, 2010; Kutash et al., 2014; Malone et al., 2007). A growing number of studies have also explored the use of MDTs to address mobilization toward violent extremist activity and violence prevention more broadly (e.g., Eisenman and Flavahan, 2017; Weine, Eisenman, et al., 2017). A portion of this research stems from a growing awareness that security measures and law enforcement–focused strategies to identify and respond to violent extremist activity and violence more generally are insufficient. highlights the need for more strategic, inclusive, and preventive approaches (Weine, Masters, and Tartaglia, 2015). The principal conclusion across this literature is that diverse sets of expertise are likelier to be effective at addressing specific risks and preventing violence when they are applied in concert and in a coordinated and reinforcing manner. For similar reasons, various sources have also highlighted that MDTs are a preferred approach to TA and threat management in schools (Atkinson, 2002; Dwyer and Osher, 2000; NTAC, 2018).

In school TA models that rely on MDTs, the members assessing threats come from different backgrounds and expertise, which can also mean that individual members come to the table with different approaches and assumptions. Different people might also need to adhere to specific legal requirements—for example, those pertaining to information-sharing. This can pose unique challenges, some of which could affect the extent to which someone is willing to come forward with information. For instance, research shows that it is often difficult to strike a balance between privacy and information-sharing within MDTs, particularly between non–law enforcement agencies and police services (Rosand, 2018). This means that the MDT model in general requires significant trust-building between community and government groups, public safety and non–public safety agencies, and other stakeholders involved in the TA process. In addition to establishing interagency trust (i.e., internal to the

MDT), gaining and sustaining the trust of local communities (i.e., external trust) can present a significant barrier to implementation and sustainment, particularly if a community has had negative experiences with members of the MDTs in the past (Ellis and Abdi, 2017). The composition of school TA teams (i.e., who is involved in evaluating a particular situation and determining appropriate follow-up actions and the external partners a school brings into its TA process) can affect students' overall trust in the TA process and ultimately their willingness to report concerning behavior.

Recent lessons learned in the wake of school shootings confirm that trusting relationships within the school—for example, among the principal, assistant principal, school counselors, SRO, and teachers—as well as relationships that exist between the school and outside agencies and service systems, such as mental health providers, social services, local police services, and families, are crucial to identifying, assessing, and managing students who might be on a path toward violence (Fein et al., 2004; Goodrum and Woodward, 2016). In the broader violence prevention literature, the research calls attention to the positive role that *local* practitioners from various fields—including local police services—play in promoting trust-based networks (Ellis, Miller, et al., 2020).

Providing Transparency into Reporting Outcomes

Michael Planty and his colleagues recommended that, to help schools build trust in their reporting programs and reassure community members that reports are taken seriously, tip line programs disseminate various statistics, such as the number and types of tips received and specific actions taken, via annual and other types of reports (Planty, Banks, Cutbush, et al., 2018). The literature also offers that schools can provide information to their communities about how the TA process itself works, such as by publishing statistics on the frequency of TA team meetings, information about who is on the team, and information about how situations have been resolved (Cornell and Maeng, 2020). Publicly available statistics about the number and types of tips received through a tip line can increase public awareness of the effects of threat reporting and TA. Without additional insight into what happened as a result of tips, concerns about a program could worsen, rather than improve. For example, without clear reporting on how a school addressed tips that it received, someone might assume that all of the tips were forwarded to law enforcement or that the school did nothing with the information. Publishing statistics on how the school actually followed up on information it received, such as referring people to mental health services in some cases and reaching out to law enforcement in others, can help avoid people making misplaced assumptions about reporting outcomes.

Indeed, communicating with the school community about the possible outcomes of reporting information is an important step, insofar as more knowledge about the downstream effects of reporting can increase people's propensity to come forward with information about concerning behavior. The literature encourages schools to communicate to students that they will not face negative consequences if they reach out to authority figures with information (Pollack, Modzeleski, and Rooney, 2008; Stueve et al., 2006). Tailored messaging can also work to change attitudes about reporting, such as in contexts in which seeking help to prevent violence equates to snitching for personal gain (Eliot et al., 2010; Stohlman and Cornell, 2019). Some studies suggest targeted, peer-education initiatives with small groups of students who are less likely to report concerning behavior as potentially viable solutions to improve reporting (Hodges et al., 2016).

Summary and Conclusions from the Literature

The literature highlights multiple challenges with threat reporting systems that influence willingness to report in K–12 school settings. One of the most-salient issues with threat reporting overall is gaining trust—trust that the reporter's identity will remain unknown and trust in the actions taken in follow-up to a report. Existing research stresses the significance of positive student–teacher and student–school staff relationships, which is not a feature of a reporting system per se but is critically important in promoting students' willingness to report. Another theme that emerged from the literature is the relationship between student demographics and reporting: Students are likelier to report concerning behavior in primary than in secondary grades and in advantaged than economically disadvantaged schools. As a result, there is likely an onus on schools serving disadvantaged communities to provide extraclear communications to students about what they can and should report, how they can do so, and potential repercussions of reporting. These and other strategies can help to address scenarios around which distrust often discourages reporting.

Although no quantitative or qualitative study to date has directly investigated the relationship between reporting program processes and procedures and student willingness to report threats, research suggests that maintaining the confidentiality of individuals who come forward with information, providing accessible reporting platforms, and building awareness of reporting programs (including increasing knowledge about the type of behaviors to report) are important features of reporting systems. The literature frequently highlights the need for formal training that is tailored to various groups of the reporting community, including students, parents, teachers, noninstructional school staff, and administrators, and the TA team itself (e.g., tip line operators, law enforcement). However, it is not clear which approaches or formats are most important for effectively building awareness and encouraging reporting, particularly among students.

CHAPTER THREE

Approaches to Threat Reporting in the K–12 School Community

The literature highlights the importance of positive school climates, cultures of trust, and certain features of reporting systems, such as anonymity and accessibility in supporting student decisions to come forward with concerns, for effective threat reporting. To learn more, we interviewed K–12 district and school leaders across the United States, as well as state-level stakeholders, to better understand contemporary approaches to building trust and encouraging reporting, as well as the challenges that schools face in this arena. In this chapter, we summarize findings from a series of interviews conducted in early 2022 with various representatives from the K–12 school community.

Interview Sample and Protocol

We took a purposive sampling approach to selecting our interview participants, seeking to include variation across contexts, such as geographic location (across the United States as well as urban, suburban, and rural locales), school district size, grade levels served, and reporting system structure. From January through April 2022, we conducted 26 interviews with 35 people involved in school safety at the state, county, community, school district, and individual school levels. Interview participants represented 13 different school districts or regional agencies across nine U.S. states.[1] Eleven of these districts served grades K–12, and two served a smaller subset of grades (grades 7 through 12 and grades K through 6). Ten districts were categorized by the National Center for Education Statistics as suburb locales, two as cities, and one as a rural locale. The smallest individual district in our sample served approximately 400 students, and the largest served more than 145,000 students.

At the state level, we conducted interviews with people responsible for managing established state-level tip lines used by districts and schools in those states. At the conclusion of each of our interviews with state-level personnel, we asked for referrals to districts in that state that could speak to district- and school-level experiences with specific reporting programs.

---

[1] The research team completed one interview with a regional education service agency serving 42 school districts and more than 100,000 students.

In addition, we reached out to school districts in other states in an effort to interview people with experience with a broader variety of reporting programs (i.e., those not managed by states), such as community-level (e.g., municipal- or county-level) threat reporting programs or district-level reporting programs. We also sought to interview people from school districts that did not use formal reporting programs, such as tip lines. Over the course of our interviews, we spoke with managers of state-level tip lines and other representatives from state school safety offices; school district safety and security personnel; district superintendents; municipal law enforcement personnel; county mental health professionals, school counselors; and assistant principals. Ultimately, our final sample size for interviews was determined by saturation (i.e., when no new information surfaced through additional interviews),[2] as well as interviewee responsiveness and availability. Figure 3.1 provides a visual overview of the geographies and locales covered in our interviews, and Table 3.1 provides a breakdown of interview participants.

FIGURE 3.1

Geographic Locations of Participants

NOTE: Markers indicate the categories of entities that interviewees represented.

_____

2 For a discussion of saturation in qualitative research, see Saunders et al., 2018.

TABLE 3.1

Interview Participants, by Role

Stakeholder Level	Number of Interviewees
State	9
District[a]	18
School	6
County	1
City	1

[a] Includes an interview with a representative from a regional education service agency.

We used a semistructured interview protocol, reproduced in the appendix, to learn about the experiences of states, districts, and schools with designing and implementing threat reporting programs, receiving reports, managing reporting processes, and encouraging reporting more generally. We took typed notes during each interview, which addressed the following topics:

- description of reporting options in place (formal and informal)
- processes for fielding reports
- the role of law enforcement in a reporting program
- outreach and training for staff, students, and families
- key system features that support or challenge reporting
- main challenges and barriers to reporting
- best practices and strategies to support reporting.

Given restrictions on travel associated with the COVID-19 pandemic, we conducted all interviews virtually via video- or teleconference. Each interview lasted approximately one hour and was conducted on a voluntary and confidential basis. The findings summarized herein reflect the perceptions of adult stakeholders from the K–12 school community. Note that, although several interview participants described student perceptions of reporting in their communities, we did not directly speak with students.

Student Concerns Around Reporting

Our conversations with stakeholders in the K–12 school community highlighted barriers that students face in reporting various types of concerns, including threats to school safety. Stakeholders' perceptions at the individual school, district, and state levels largely confirmed findings from the literature, stressing that some of the largest barriers to reporting are such factors as fear of retribution, being labeled a snitch, school or law enforcement actions in response to tips, and more-general concerns about anonymity.

Across our interviews, school, district, and state-level personnel involved in school safety reported perceiving student concerns about anonymity to be a significant hindrance to reporting. Interview participants said that students tended to have low levels of trust even in anonymous reporting programs; they said that students expressed their suspicions that school administrators or others receiving the tip would not maintain a reporter's anonymity or that the details they provided in their tips would be traceable back to them. For instance, one stakeholder told us, "The biggest thing for students is anonymity. . . . When you say to them that they don't have to give their name, they'll still have concerns about being identified via their IP address."[3] Tip lines that are limited to phone numbers tend to feel especially identifiable, according to one stakeholder.[4]

Moreover, interview participants reported believing that a student considering submitting a tip worries both about being labeled a snitch and about retribution or retaliation that might occur as a result of reporting. Often, students simply preferred, interviewees said, to stay out of situations that they perceived could get them or a friend in trouble or to stay quiet to avoid perceptions that they had betrayed a friendship. Some stakeholders highlighted the negative role that peer pressure can play when it comes to reporting; in some contexts, for example, students seen walking into an administrator's office are immediately assumed to either be tattling or in trouble, they said.[5] Stakeholders said that these barriers are magnified in contexts with high gang presence or when cultural norms around reporting deter students from coming forward with information about peers' concerning behavior.[6] Overall, our interviews suggest that environments in which students do not feel safe sharing their concerns pose a significant barrier to reporting.

In some cases, our interviewees said that students can be discouraged from reporting when they believe that their information will not be taken seriously or lead to negative consequences for either themselves or their friends. As one district representative explained, "Students didn't want to get friends in trouble [by reporting them]." Disclosing a peer's struggle with mental health, or fear that a certain offense might lead to law enforcement involvement or remain on someone's record for the long term, are notable deterrents to reporting. On the other hand, school administrators' failure to follow up can also discourage students from reporting their concerns; as one county-level stakeholder noted, "Many students feel that, even if they do report [something] to their school, nothing happens."[7] And in many cases, interview participants said that students simply do not know or are confused about what type of behavior they should report and so refrain from doing so entirely; district and school per-

---

[3] Interview with district-level stakeholder, March 2022.

[4] Interview with district-level stakeholder, March 2022.

[5] Interview with school-level stakeholder, March 2022.

[6] Interviews with state-level stakeholder, February 2022; school-level stakeholders, February and March 2022; and district-level stakeholder, February 2022.

[7] Interview with county-level stakeholder, February 2022.

sonnel expressed that students often perceive their peers' behavior to be "a joke" or as harmless, even when intentions are, in reality, more serious.

Our interviews also reinforced a key finding highlighted in the literature review in the importance of trust and relationships in the decision about whether to report (see, e.g., Pollack, Modzeleski, and Rooney, 2008). District and school personnel stressed that trusting relationships between students and staff at school encourage reporting. When these relationships are weak or altogether absent, they said, students are less likely to report concerns. According to some interview participants, the importance of climates of trust also extends to students' home lives: Students who have consistent access to trusted adults both at home and at school are likelier to speak up when they have concerns.[8]

Finally, interview participants expressed a variety of views on whether the involvement of law enforcement—including SROs—in the TA and threat reporting process influences students' propensity to come forward with information. According to some district- and school-level stakeholders, some parents who have negative views of police have discouraged their kids from reporting.[9] A parent's concern about a reporting program can also stem from a misunderstanding of law enforcement's role in school disciplinary issues, such as when the parent mistakenly believes that police will contribute to responding to noncriminal student behavior, such as bullying, which is more typically addressed by school administrators.[10] These misconceptions can negatively influence students' perceptions of reporting programs and ultimately highlight the importance of outreach and training on reporting programs.

Other concerns focused more on law enforcement's ability to integrate into the school community and gain students' trust; our interview participants said that law enforcement personnel who have strong relationships with students are likelier to encourage reporting and become trusted adults with whom students feel comfortable sharing their concerns. To this end, interviewees stressed the importance of the training that SROs and school police officers receive, along with everyday efforts to build rapport with the broader school community. For example, one district-level representative from a large urban district noted that that district trains its officers "on [school-specific] skills and requirements, emphasizing that they are a resource for students."[11] SROs who receive only general law enforcement training, not school-specific training, are less likely to play a role in encouraging students to report concerning behavior.[12] Moreover, SROs who participated in our interviews said that students are likelier

---

[8]   Interviews with district-level stakeholders, February and March 2022.

[9]   Interviews with school-level stakeholder, March 2022, and district-level stakeholder, March 2022.

[10] Interview with district-level stakeholder, March 2022.

[11] Interview with district-level stakeholder, February 2022.

[12] The National Association of SROs provides a series of training courses designed for law enforcement officers and school safety personnel who work with school administrations. The courses focus on building "positive relationships with both students and staff," helping SROs better "identify and respond to students who are suspected of having a mental health need," and other topics (National Association of SROs, undated).

to view law enforcement officers who make deliberate and consistent efforts to be involved—for example, by attending sporting or other community events—as another group of people who are willing to help in troubling times: "It's the little things, like walking around, holding doors open, attending graduation . . . that gains us trust."[13]

In noting these concerns, the stakeholders who participated in our research stressed the need to educate students about the importance of reporting and to establish positive climates for reporting, whether through informal approaches, such as trust-building, or more-formal programs, such as the establishment of anonymous tip lines. In the case of these latter tip line–based approaches, demonstrating anonymity is almost as important as establishing the program itself, given student concerns about "being found out." The next section presents these approaches as discussed by our interviewees and highlights some of the challenges that schools and districts have faced in encouraging reporting.

Strategies and Approaches to Threat Reporting

In line with studies that demonstrate the importance that reporting has in preventing targeted violence in schools (e.g., Stallings and Hall, 2019; Vossekuil et al., 2004), our interview participants across the state, district, and school levels agreed that supporting students in coming forward with information is critical to fostering safe school environments. Across the 13 districts and regional units represented in our interview sample, stakeholders unanimously stressed reporting's importance to enhancing school safety and, at a minimum, described ongoing efforts to encourage students to report directly to a trusted adult. Nine of the 13 districts employed formal threat reporting systems, such as a statewide, districtwide, or countywide anonymous tip line. In addition, three districts noted their use of social media or network monitoring tools, such as Bark or Gaggle, which flag content containing pre-identified target words, such as "gun" or "suicide." Four districts included in our sample did not use a formal reporting system at the time of our interviews, although one was preparing for the near-term implementation of a communication application that would allow school staff to report various needs related to school safety (e.g., support for managing a disruptive student or suspicious behavior). Table 3.2 provides an overview of the various approaches to threat reporting represented in our sample.

Across all of our interviews, stakeholders emphasized the importance of fostering a climate of trust grounded in strong relationships as the foundation of a positive reporting culture, echoing findings from the literature. As one district-level stakeholder noted, "You can't have an effective [reporting] program with an app alone; you must live it in the climate and culture. And if you don't respond in a timely manner, kids won't believe and trust you."[14] Interview participants repeatedly referenced the need for staff to establish rapport and build

---

[13] Interview with school-level stakeholder, March 2022.

[14] Interview with district-level stakeholder, March 2022.

TABLE 3.2

Breakdown of Tip Line Use Across Represented Districts

Category	Districts
District-level tip line	5
State-level tip line	3
Combination state- and district-level tip line	1
No formal tip line	4

trust with students as a way of increasing willingness to report. For example, another district-level stakeholder stressed that schools "need rapport building and trusting relationships. Those who are successful [at encouraging reporting] are the schools with visible staff, those who are sitting with students at lunch and greeting them at arrival."[15] An SRO assigned to a high school echoed this sentiment:

> The most critical thing [in building rapport] is being visible and present and actively engaging with kids. . . . When you walk by them playing, ask them how it's going, what their interests are. Find common ground and build mutual respect, be approachable, not just standing around monitoring.[16]

The nine districts that use state-, district-, or countywide reporting programs offer additional avenues for their student population and members of the broader school community to submit tips, beyond going directly to a trusted adult. As one district staff commented, "You must have [multiple methods for reporting]. It's one of the top best practices when it comes to school security."[17] These additional avenues include phone numbers, web portals, and mobile applications that include live-dialogue features. A key feature in many of these platforms is the option for someone to provide information anonymously, which is not an option when a student reports information directly to a school administrator, school law enforcement, counselor, or other adult. Given the significant concerns students have about being labeled a snitch or about potential retaliation, interviewees across the schools and districts represented in our sample highlighted anonymity as a significant benefit of student tip lines. As one district-level stakeholder noted, the "anonymous platform is just another layer of reporting. It gives that one fraction of the community who prefers to remain anonymous the ability to do so and still bring information forward."[18] Another district-level stakeholder stressed the need

---

[15] Interview with district-level stakeholder, March 2022.

[16] Interview with school-level stakeholder, March 2022.

[17] Interview with district level stakeholder, March 2022.

[18] Interview with district-level stakeholder, March 2022.

for an anonymous reporting method "even if there are strong relationships between students and staff, because sometimes there's a fear of saying something out loud."[19]

Interview participants described a handful of additional tip line features that appealed to them insofar as they supported efforts to increase student willingness to report. These included the following:

- features related to user experience and accessibility, such as the availability of various reporting platforms and overall ease of use of a web portal or mobile application. Stakeholders said that these features made reporting easier for students and the broader reporting community.
- making a program available to the reporting community 24 hours per day, seven days per week
- contracting a third party to operate a tip line program to further encourage reporting and take some of the burden off school staff. As one district-level representative noted,

  the biggest plus [about our program] is the 24/7 call center to manage threats and triage [tips] to schools. The district doesn't have capacity to do this. . . . It's very expensive to have a team trained up to manage a tip line at the district level.[20]

- integrating live-dialogue options that allow a person who is reporting to communicate directly with a responding party and to provide additional details to bolster their report, all while maintaining their anonymity. In these programs, tip line operators who converse with reporters—either via phone or online chat—receive specialized training as crisis counselors or other crisis-intervention experts. One district-level stakeholder noted that, through their program, managed by Sandy Hook Promise's Say Something Anonymous reporting system, "You get trained counselors with crisis counseling knowledge and education. They know how to work with kids, and their training and experience is important."[21]
- features allowing reporters to upload photos and screenshots to provide more-detailed information that could further enable response.
- features that help catalogue and track responses to tips. Many established reporting programs, such as Say Something Anonymous, include structured systems for managing triage and response to tips:

  A system that integrates good notes about what happened in response to a tip is important. You need to be able to reassure kids that their concerns are going to be taken seriously,

---

[19] Interview with district-level stakeholder, February 2022.

[20] Interview with district-level stakeholder, March 2022.

[21] Interview with district-level stakeholder, March 2022.

that you'll do something with their information. In this regard, actions speak louder than words.[22]

The four districts that did not operate or use a tip line did so for various reasons. One district serving only grades K–6 did not believe that a tip line would add significant value as far as school safety was concerned because young students are likelier than older students to go directly to their teachers with any concerns.[23] Representatives of another district, a small rural one serving fewer than 400 students, told us that their tightly knit network of staff and students precluded the need for a tip line: "We have such dynamic staff—kids think they can talk to any teacher. Our network is so strong, so we haven't reached out to establish a tip line."[24] Conversely, representatives from another district serving more than 140,000 students expressed concerned that the implementation of a formal reporting system might further overwhelm staff who are already required to respond to high levels of classroom disruption; nevertheless, these stakeholders did recognize the benefits that an anonymous reporting process could introduce, were one to be implemented.[25] These responses suggest that reasons for implementing reporting such programs as tip lines rather than relying exclusively on informal approaches to reporting, such as building a trusting school climate, are often context-specific.

In sum, our interviews suggest that various tip line features work to build trust and promote a culture of reporting within schools. In addition to revealing the focus on building trusting environments that foster strong reporting climates, our conversations with stakeholders in the K–12 school community stressed that the ability to report anonymously is one of the more important features that a school can provide to its student population to increase willingness to report. Moreover, increasing avenues for reporting beyond just sharing information with a trusted adult provides further support; our interview participants said that, when students also have the option to report concerning behavior via their phones or computers, they are likelier to come forward with information.

Receiving and Fielding Reports

As noted in previous sections, options to receive and field reports provided through tip lines vary across reporting programs and schools; our interviews further highlighted this diversity. Our conversations with state-, district-, and school-level school safety personnel revealed that tip lines utilize a wide variety of people to answer reports, including external analysts employed by a private reporting program, state-employed analysts, county or municipal law enforcement personnel, and school staff. For instance, in districts that use the Sandy Hook

---

[22] Interview with school-level stakeholder, March 2022.

[23] Interview with district-level stakeholder, March 2022.

[24] Interview with district-level stakeholder, April 2022.

[25] Interview with district-level stakeholder, February 2022.

Promise Say Something Anonymous reporting system, operators trained and employed by Sandy Hook Promise interact with the person reporting and then triage the report to a state, district, or school team as determined by state or district protocols.[26] In districts that use the Anonymous Alerts reporting system, a local school administrator, such as an assistant principal, engages directly with the person submitting the report and subsequently triages that information to a team as determined by district protocols. In the nine districts included in our sample that used formal tip lines, reports were forwarded directly to school law enforcement, such as an SRO, in only four cases. County-level law enforcement officials managed the school tip line for one of the districts represented in our sample; in this district, the reporter provided information directly to local law enforcement personnel, who then forwarded information to the district's safety and security team.[27]

Processes to triage information provided through a tip line also varied across the districts in our sample, particularly with respect to local law enforcement involvement. For example, state-level representatives from two states noted that statute mandated that they forward all incoming reports to relevant district, school, and local law enforcement personnel; however, none of those personnel were involved in answering tip lines.[28] In fact, a representative from another state told us that they deliberately employ non–law enforcement personnel to answer tip lines and triage information to avoid perceptions that police are directly involved in receiving and tracking tips.[29] In many of our interviews, stakeholders noted that the main benefit of law enforcement involvement in receiving information provided through a tip line is the capability for 24/7 response. In most cases, law enforcement becomes involved in follow-up action only if a tip provides information about criminal activity or life-safety events.

Following Up on Tips

A review of the literature and interviews with stakeholders in the K–12 school community suggests that student concerns about follow-up actions taken in the aftermath of submitting a tip can discourage reporting. In fact, several interview participants explicitly cited visible follow-up in response to tips as important to encouraging reporting; they said that actions taken by school administrators and other partners—as well as consistency in those actions—demonstrate accountability and build credibility with students. As one district representative stated, a "reporting system doesn't mean much if you don't have a follow-up process."[30]

---

[26] Interviews with state-level stakeholder, January 2022, and with district-level stakeholder, March 2022.

[27] Interview with district-level stakeholder, March 2022.

[28] Interview with state-level stakeholders, January and February 2022.

[29] Interview with state-level stakeholder, January 2022.

[30] Interview with district-level stakeholder, March 2022.

Stakeholders also indicated that actions speak louder than words when it comes to making students feel safe reporting:

> The most critical thing for students to come forward is the relationships that they have with the people at the school and confidence that, if they tell a teacher about their worries, they trust [that] it is going to be handled the right way. For them, it's less about how things are messaged than about how they see the school react.[31]

Nevertheless, although interviewees cited response follow-up as a key strategy to encourage reporting, several districts reported challenges related to limited staff capacity. One district representative stated, "[The] biggest challenge is finding the resources to respond to all the tips. It takes time to coordinate . . . but the return on investment for this program is life. It's big."[32]

To better understand these dynamics, we asked stakeholders in the K–12 school community about who is involved in responding to tips and what steps districts and schools take in response to tips, including TAs (which are sometimes enacted in response to tips). Generally speaking, each district or school included in our sample involved at least one school administrator and a school counselor in TA and threat response; some teams also included a law enforcement representative, such as a school police officer or SRO. Notably, SRO involvement in the TA process varied. In one state, for example, the decision to include an SRO, as well as other student-support personnel, such as a clinician, school psychologist, or social worker, on a TA team is left to individual districts.[33] In other states and districts represented in our sample, every LEA included a school security officer or an SRO or both on its TA team.

Some of our interview participants highlighted the important role that they said that SROs and school police can play in increasing student willingness to report. For instance, one state-level stakeholder told us, "students are more likely to view the SRO as part of the school community [than to have that view of] law enforcement at large. Not all of our districts have SROs, but students in those with SROs [are likelier to] trust reporting."[34] This sentiment reflects findings from the literature that law enforcement officers (e.g., SROs) assigned to schools can play a unique role in promoting student willingness to report threats, provided that they gain the trust of the broader school community—students in particular (Cornell, 2020). District- and school-level stakeholders from other states also said that SROs and school police officers can help reduce student concerns and encourage reporting: "If anything, the

---

[31] Interview with city-level stakeholder, January 2022.

[32] Interview with district-level interviewee, March 2022.

[33] Interview with district-level stakeholder, February 2022.

[34] Interview with state-level stakeholder, February 2022.

potential for school police involvement might actually bring relief that other people are going to get involved. Kids in general here feel safer when [school] law enforcement is there."[35]

Findings from our interviews suggest that the extent to which law enforcement is beneficial to reporting is context-dependent, varying with such factors as characteristics of the student body. As one school-level stakeholder explained, "We have lots of law enforcement and military families here and at this particular school; kids are receptive to help from the SRO. But in other counties, involving the SRO could deter reporting."[36] In contrast with the district-level stakeholder who referred to the potential for an SRO to serve as a reassuring presence in school settings, others said that uniformed personnel can be intimidating to some students, whom they said preferred to turn to other trusted adults with their concerns.[37] One district-level representative referenced their need to shift away from a county-level reporting system operated by a local law enforcement agency, explaining that the reporting system essentially "linked behavior to crime" and aggravated student fears about the potential impact of reporting.[38] The ensuing implementation of a school-managed anonymous reporting system, which accounted for students' fears, helped promote tip lines as direct supports to students.[39]

Approaches to Outreach and Building Awareness

Threat reporting is an effective violence prevention tool in K–12 schools insofar as students and members of the broader reporting community are aware of available resources (see e.g., Cornell and Maeng, 2020; Hodges et al., 2016; Stohlman and Cornell, 2019). To this end, some interview participants stressed the importance of building awareness of reporting. Stakeholders in the K–12 school community employ a variety of outreach and training strategies to broaden awareness, including developing marketing materials, such as flyers and presentations; formal training targeting various members of the reporting community; and engaging student groups. In all of these diverse strategies, the goal is to convey information about the importance and impact of reporting, what to report (e.g., threats of violence, violent ideations, crime- and drug-related issues), the various avenues through which someone can report information, specific features of the reporting program, and what happens after a report is received.

---

[35] Interview with school-level stakeholder, March 2022. Of note is that these findings are based on the opinions of school and district staff, who were describing their impressions of student perceptions of SROs, school police, and other law enforcement entities. We did not ask students about their perceptions of school or other law enforcement entities.

[36] Interview with school-level stakeholder, March 2022.

[37] Interview with district-level stakeholder, March 2022.

[38] Interview with district-level stakeholder, February 2022.

[39] Interview with district-level stakeholder, February 2022.

The majority of interview participants referenced multiple marketing and outreach tools as part of their strategies to build awareness around reporting. Some of the approaches highlighted by stakeholders included the following:

- displaying information about reporting on posters, through quick-response (QR) codes, or on pens, lanyards, or the backs of staff and student identification cards
- disseminating information about reporting via schoolwide emails, newsletters, and district and school websites
- spreading information about reporting through school and district social media accounts. Many state-level school safety agencies or other partners engaged in threat reporting are also active on various social media platforms, such as Twitter and Instagram.
- disseminating information about reporting during major school events, such as all-school assemblies, back-to-school nights, or parent–teacher association meetings.
- implementing training on reporting for students, teachers, administrators, and other school staff throughout the school year. Our interviews confirmed that most outreach and training efforts target students, followed by school staff, and then parents and other members of the broader reporting community.

Student Training and Outreach

Most of the messaging on student-facing reporting stresses the importance of reporting and addresses student concerns and fears about consequences. For example, messaging strategies described in our interviews frame reporting and any follow-up interventions as ways for students to help their peers, stressing that it is everyone's responsibility to keep the school community safe. As one interview participant noted about the reporting system in place in their district,

> students fear the impacts that reporting something might have on students' education plans or employment. . . . We address these fears by explaining the process. We emphasize that we have a stand-alone reporting system that's not linked to law enforcement, and we only go to law enforcement for life crisis situations.[40]

Another district-level stakeholder told us that their messaging on reporting stresses, "It is a supportive process available to all students. . . . [We] stress equity and the fact that [TA] meetings are set up to understand and support [students], not punish."[41]

To reduce confusion about reporting, outreach with students also focuses heavily on what to report. As one district-level stakeholder stressed, "It's important to make the reporting threshold clear. Students typically don't realize how important the information they're pro-

---

[40] Interview with district-level stakeholder, February 2022.

[41] Interview with district-level stakeholder, February 2022.

viding actually is, they think adults already know or probably know."[42] Other interview participants said that, although many students can recognize a friend in trouble, they are often unsure about whether a behavior warrants reporting. Training and outreach that aim to help students recognize clear warning signs are thus valuable tools to support student reporting.

Interviewees described multiple approaches to provide training and outreach to students. For example, one state-level stakeholder described the implementation of differentiated trainings for students according to grade level and based on the demands of school schedules.[43] Other state- or district-level stakeholders who used private reporting systems, such as Sandy Hook Promise's Say Something Anonymous program, used premade trainings for students of various ages, sometimes tailoring the material to make it more specific to their school context. For example, one school-level stakeholder noted, "We showed the kids the video early on, and [they were not responsive]. You have to have some flexibility and find the methods to gain students' attention that work for [your students]."[44] Other districts modified premade training videos to remove certain types of content, such as what they considered to be overly violent imagery, or to insert the voices of school staff to make the material appear more familiar to students. Additional strategies have included developing trainings that explain the importance of reporting through storytelling, which might be more effective for some types of learners.

Typically, students receive longer training on the importance of reporting at the beginning of the school year and shorter refresher trainings at various points throughout the school year. This helps keep the information fresh in their minds and remind them of the tools and resources available to them for reporting. In fact, our interview participants expressed agreement that training and outreach focusing on various reporting topics did have a notable impact on reporting: Some school- and district-level stakeholders told us that the number of received reports was often higher in periods immediately following training or outreach events, then dropped off as time passed.[45] Nevertheless, as a reporting program becomes more engrained into a school's everyday practices, formal outreach efforts, such as training, become less necessary. In one district where a state-level reporting program had been in place for more than a decade, a district-level stakeholder told us, "Initially, we visited every classroom; it was a big lift. The program is now so well-known in this district that even elementary school kids know about it."[46]

Across many of our district- and school-level interviews, stakeholders agreed that formal training on tip lines using the strategies described above is especially important beginning in middle school (i.e., at around the sixth-grade level). Nevertheless, some schools and districts

---

[42] Interview with district-level stakeholder, February 2022.

[43] Interview with state-level stakeholder, January 2022.

[44] Interview with school-level stakeholder, March 2022.

[45] Interviews with district-level stakeholder, February 2022, and with school-level stakeholder, March 2022.

[46] Interview with district-level stakeholder, March 2022.

included in our sample did introduce tip line programs to elementary schools, given the reality that many elementary-age children now bring phones to school.[47] In elementary schools, outreach efforts focus more on instilling the message of "being a good friend," especially in lower grades, such as kindergarten through second.[48] Overall, stakeholders agreed on the importance of building awareness of reporting early on in students' minds:

> We try to make sure that we invest, particularly at the elementary level, in a trusting and supportive climate and culture. . . . If you build a culture and climate where people feel it's safe to talk about health and other needs, and it's not considered snitching or weakness, reporting will happen naturally.[49]

Peer-to-Peer Outreach

Several school-, district-, and state-level interviewees in our sample also directly referenced engaging students in outreach efforts on reporting. As one state-level stakeholder commented, "Getting students enlisted in the work is important. They are going to either champion it or subvert it, so having student voices behind [a reporting program], in the codesign of it, is important."[50]

Indeed, some student tip lines in place at the state level formally include student-led outreach efforts as part of their strategy to build awareness of reporting. For instance, one state in our interview sample regularly engaged a student focus group to inform decisionmaking around reporting; plans are underway to expand participation in this focus group to each county in the state.[51] Another state-level stakeholder described the formation of a student ambassador program for high school students; these students provide feedback on marketing materials and social media campaigns with an eye toward designing and launching material that will appeal to students.[52]

Outside of formal engagement efforts, such as those described above, representatives from four districts in our sample told us that they asked students for input on materials and messaging on reporting and that they asked students to directly engage with their peers to spread information about reporting programs. One district-level stakeholder described that each school in the district had a student club that focused on efforts to prevent school violence; the district engaged student members in refresher training on reporting and to help build

---

[47] Interview with district-level stakeholder, March 2022.

[48] Interview with district-level stakeholder, March 2022.

[49] Interview with district-level stakeholder, March 2022.

[50] Interview with state-level stakeholder, February 2022.

[51] Interview with state-level stakeholder, January 2022.

[52] Interview with state-level stakeholder, February 2022.

connections with students who had faced disciplinary action in the past.[53] Other interview participants referenced efforts to engage existing student clubs to inform their peers and lead discussions around school safety topics, including how to identify concerning behavior.[54] As one interviewee noted, "It hits an adolescent differently [when they hear it] from a peer, rather than someone their parents' age telling them about [the tip line]."[55]

Outreach to the Broader Reporting Community

In addition to students, targets of outreach and training on reporting include school staff and other members of the community, such as parents. When support for and implementation of reporting programs is uneven across a particular state or individual school district, these engagements are especially important. Outreach with staff, for example, is crucial in promoting buy-in for reporting programs; when school staff show active support for a program, they are likelier to successfully play a role in encouraging and supporting students to report. Findings from our interviews suggest that garnering strong buy-in from school leadership is especially important, insofar as it helps to promote a strong school culture of reporting, future outreach efforts, and recognition that school staff themselves play a crucial role in the process. As one school-level stakeholder noted, it is often necessary to use a "top-down approach for onboarding [a reporting program] and collecting buy-in. [You] need the principal's [buy-in] before you get the teachers' and the students.'"[56]

It is also important to ensure that school staff follow specific protocols related to reporting, such as maintaining reporters' anonymity and promptly following up on reports and tips. These latter dynamics are themselves critical to supporting students who want to come forward with information; if school staff are not aware of their roles and responsibilities in the reporting process, students will be likelier to be unwilling to report concerning behavior directly to them. Interviewees highlighted the importance of staff training, particularly when launching a new program: "It took a lot of training for the schools. They needed to know how to identify the warning behaviors and then where to go with that information. We did a lot of trainings at the beginning."[57] Schools and districts have found that setting time aside to talk specifically about reporting (for example, during staff training days) is critical to gaining staff's attention and the necessary buy-in to make a program successful.[58]

Finally, interview participants noted that informing parents and guardians about existing reporting systems and associated processes is also important. For the most part, the stakeholders with whom we spoke saw parents as playing a role in helping to foster a culture of

---

[53] Interview with district-level stakeholder, March 2022.

[54] Interviews with district-level stakeholders, February and March 2022.

[55] Interview with district-level stakeholder, February 2022.

[56] Interview with school-level stakeholder, March 2022.

[57] Interview with county-level stakeholder, February 2022.

[58] Interview with school-level stakeholder, March 2022.

reporting at home. Outreach targeting parents focused primarily on explaining the features of a reporting system (such as anonymity and the various platforms available to file a report) and learning how to recognize concerning behavior. Most efforts targeting parents described in our interviews involved general marketing outreach (for example, via social media messaging or school or district websites). A handful of districts in our sample also send families written materials that describe the approach to reporting (in, e.g., back-to-school packets, brochures, parent letters) or present relevant material at parent–teacher association meetings or community events. A strategy that many of our interview participants emphasized was communication saturation, or the constant dissemination of reminders to the reporting community about the importance of reporting or a particular reporting program. As one stakeholder noted, "We market on everything we can think of. . . . We made it a part of our culture for so many years [that] even parents remember it from when they were in school."[59]

Together, these training and outreach efforts contribute to increasing students' awareness of the resources available to them for reporting. The efforts also promote and encourage reporting insofar as they teach students how to identify behaviors that should be reported, and they often work to allay concerns about what happens after submitting a report. Training and outreach that target school staff work to further support students seeking to report, especially when training emphasizes protecting reporters' identities and explains to students that the school will take their information seriously and follow up appropriately.

---

[59] Interview with district-level stakeholder, March 2022.

CHAPTER FOUR

Conclusions and Implications for the K–12 School Community

Our review of the literature and interview data point to a consensus that threat reporting is a critical component of school violence prevention efforts. Nationwide, schools and school districts emphasize the importance of cultures of trust and strong relationships between students and staff to encourage reporting, and many have established structured tip line systems that allow students, parents, staff, and other members of the community to provide information about potential threats.

Despite the impact that reporting can have on preventing school violence and the various platforms that are available to students and others seeking to share information, many people still feel reluctant to come forward. Fears of being labeled a snitch or of potential retaliation limit students' willingness to report. Others do not trust adults with keeping their information confidential or acting on their information or are uncomfortable with the potential for disciplinary action that reporting might bring. Others simply do not know what type of behavior they should report.

In response to these and other challenges, states, districts, and schools around the country have identified strategies to promote reporting. Many of these relate to efforts to improve school climate and build trust within the school community: Reducing the prevalence of aggressive student attitudes, avoiding zero-tolerance policies, and fostering a climate in which students are comfortable sharing information with adults and seeking help when they need it are all strategies cited in the literature (Eliot et al., 2010; Harrington, 2002; Millspaugh et al., 2015; Pollack, Modzeleski, and Rooney, 2008; Sulkowski, 2011; Syvertsen, Flanagan, and Stout, 2009; Unnever and Cornell, 2004; Wylie et al., 2010). In our interviews, stakeholders also stressed the importance of student–staff relationships, which extends to law enforcement officers when they are present on a school campus. Where SROs make efforts to build and sustain strong, supportive relationships with the student population, students are likely to view them as trusted adults to whom they can take a concern.

Moreover, our interviews with relevant stakeholders in the K–12 school community have shown that willingness to report threats is likely to increase when students see that their information is taken seriously and that administrators enforce school rules fairly and consistently. Indeed, communication about what happens when a school receives information about a threat is important to assuaging student fears about reporting; several studies have highlighted how the perceived credibility of the reporting process influences willingness to report concerning behavior (CSSRC, 2020; Fein et al., 2004; NTAC, 2018). Practices to build confidence in the reporting process include frequent monitoring, efficient management and processing of reports, responsiveness, and preparedness to act on reports (CSSRC, 2020; Cornell, 2011; Hollister et al., 2014; NTAC, 2018; Planty, Banks, Lindquist, et al., 2020). Without providing outcome data, or even simply publicizing established protocols for when specific tips are forwarded to law enforcement and when they are left to school-based teams to address, the assessment of reporting programs—and therefore people's willingness to report threats to a program—are based on assumptions rather than objective data. Our interviews have shown how parents' misconceptions about law enforcement involvement in school disciplinary actions, for instance, have shaped individual perceptions of the outcomes of reporting and decreased trust in a program. Although any effort to provide outcome data would have to take student privacy and other constraints into consideration, these findings show that there is nonetheless a real benefit to transparency.

Training programs that educate the reporting community—especially students—about how to submit reports (e.g., providing information about points of contact for reports, phone numbers and emails, instructions for completing online forms, instructions for accessing web and mobile application platforms), what and when to report, and what happens after someone has submitted a report are also critical to encouraging reporting. Our review of the literature and conversations with myriad stakeholders offer approaches to building awareness and knowledge of reporting, such as posters, lanyards, QR codes, and peer-to-peer training programs that help spread the word through the student population about the benefits of reporting. The more often that students, school staff, and others are reminded of the resources at their disposal for reporting, the less hesitant they are likely to be to report their concerns.

Moreover, the available research and our conversations with varied stakeholders emphasized that specific choices around the design and implementation of threat reporting programs—in particular because these concern anonymity and accessibility—are critical to supporting people who seek to report (see, e.g., Hodges et al., 2016). Although details about reporting methods, such as referrals, spoken reports, emails, and written notes submitted via comment boxes, remain vague in the literature, several studies and our interviews with stakeholders across the K–12 school community indicate benefits of offering multiple, anonymous reporting modes to increase accessibility (CSSRC, 2020; Kelly, 2018; Kenny, 2010).

Finally, we acknowledge limitations to our study, all of which have been noted previously. Most specifically, our research did not include interviews with students. Instead, it drew on conversations with adult stakeholders from the K–12 school environment, who generously offered their perspectives on when they believed that students were more or less likely to feel supported in reporting. This limitation is somewhat mitigated by the fact that studies represented in our literature review did themselves elicit student sentiments toward reporting, largely through survey-based research. Our findings reflect this research but do not provide new insight based directly on student perspectives of reporting.

Additionally, although we believe that our interview sample is representative of the approaches that various K–12 schools and districts across the United States are taking on reporting, certain perspectives might be excluded by our snowball sampling approach and limits in interviewee responsiveness and availability.

Furthermore, the lack of literature on the effectiveness of various approaches to reporting, including tip lines, precludes us from making definitive statements about what works best in preventing targeted school violence and other acts of school violence more broadly. Our findings are based on the experience of schools and districts included in our interview sample and on the findings of existing studies that capture what students would do if they observed threats and other concerning behavior. As tip lines become more prominent in U.S. K–12 schools, future research can improve our understanding of their effectiveness as a school violence prevention tool.

In summary, we highlight implications for school safety planning from our research on threat reporting and encouraging students to come forward with information:

- **Strong relationships between students and school staff are essential for building trust and robust reporting cultures.** There is no single solution to supporting people seeking to come forward with information, and solutions that work in one school context might not work well in others. Regardless of the approach in place, trusting school climates in which students feel comfortable going to an adult with their concerns are the foundation of productive approaches to reporting. Relationships between students and different members of a school's staff—including teachers, administrators, counselors, facilities managers, and SROs—are all critical to supporting students seeking to come forward with their concerns. Schools with weaker student–staff relationships can work to improve those relationships by increasing opportunities for teachers and other staff to interact with groups of students outside the classroom, such as during arrival, dismissal, and passing times and at extracurricular events, such as sports games and musical and theatrical performances. This can be especially important in contexts with low levels of community trust in police; schools in these contexts might place especially strong emphasis on training school police, SROs, and other school security personnel on school-specific skills and emphasize that they are a resource for students. Examples of relevant training topics include building positive relationships with students and school staff and identifying and responding to mental health needs.
- **Approaches to reporting are likelier to support various members of the reporting community, including students, if they emphasize accessibility and cater to ways in which today's student population communicates.** Schools and districts should work to make numerous avenues available to students and other community members who want to come forward with information. Moreover, formal programs set up to promote reporting—such as tip lines—should be widely accessible to students and the broader reporting community. A system that enables reporting via a toll-free phone number,

web portal, or mobile device application is a strong complement to in-person reporting directly to a teacher or other trusted adult.

- **An anonymous reporting option can help address student fears of being ostracized by their peers as a result of reporting.** Anonymous reporting systems allow people to submit tips without providing any information that can be used to identify them. Although anonymity poses some complications in following up on tips, the conversations that we had with diverse stakeholders in the U.S. K–12 community suggest that the benefits far outweigh the costs. Hosts of anonymous reporting systems, whether at the state, district, or school level, should clearly message to their communities whether and under what specific conditions a reporter's anonymity could potentially be forfeited. Alternatively, schools and districts can host confidential reporting systems, in which information about the reporter is collected but kept private.
- **Reporting programs that give students and others the option to speak or chat directly with an operator trained to interact with someone in crisis provide additional support to youths and can lower barriers to reporting for those not comfortable speaking directly with law enforcement.** Many state- and district-level tip lines across the country make trained operators available to reporters, in part to avoid perceptions that a reporting program is tied to law enforcement. Trained operators, such as crisis counselors, can also provide immediate support to people reporting suicidal ideation or self-harm. Schools and districts should consider their unique contexts to decide who should be responsible for fielding reports coming in through tip lines and whether they will require law enforcement support to field and triage tips (for example, in the case of tip lines available 24/7 to the reporting community).
- **Building awareness and implementing training on the importance of reporting and the means through which students can report information are critical to supporting people seeking to come forward.** Students, like anyone, are likelier to report when they are aware of the means at their disposal and know when and what to report. Regular training and outreach (for example, every two years) can help build this knowledge. Although many reporting systems make prerecorded training available to participating schools and districts, there is value to tailoring such materials to make them relevant to specific school contexts and therefore more resonant to many student bodies. Training programs that build knowledge around reporting might also consider providing short, relatable examples via scenarios or vignettes that illustrate situations or circumstances worthy of reporting. Finally, engaging students themselves in training and outreach can help lower barriers to reporting among their more-reluctant peers.
- **Transparency and communication around how schools act on information reported through a tip line or via other methods influence students' willingness to come forward.** It is important for states, districts, and schools to be transparent about the downstream effects of reporting. Annual and other periodic reports to the reporting community can increase transparency around critical issues, such as when information is shared with law enforcement and when situations are left exclusively to school

administrators. Ideally, information contained in a reporting program's annual reports would help support both the program's legitimacy (i.e., perceived fairness across different groups within the student population) and its efficacy (i.e., showing that actions are taken in response to reports). Such information can help remove or lessen what research suggests could be significant barriers to reporting and, therefore, any reporting and assessment effort's protective value. Students are also important communicators about a reporting system's downstream effects; schools can encourage those who have reported information in the past to share their experiences with their peers in an effort to reduce hesitation to report.

- **Gaining buy-in from school leadership, teachers, and other school staff is likelier to lead to an effective and sustainable reporting program.** School leaders and staff are critical to a reporting program's success. However, the introduction of new responsibilities related to reporting can place additional burdens on school staff members' time. When implementing a new program, an LEA can ease this burden by offering clear guidance on staff roles in the reporting process. Staff training offered before the start of a new school year—for instance, during new-teacher and -staff onboarding—can be a good opportunity for sharing information about a program and beginning to build buy-in across diverse staff members. LEAs can also provide teachers with teaching material related to a reporting program, making it easier for teachers to share details about a program with their students and further spread the word about the importance of reporting. Making it easier for teachers to play a role in reporting will help build buy-in for new programs and increase their longevity.

Interview Protocol

1.   BACKGROUND QUESTIONS
     We would like to begin by asking some general questions about your professional background in school safety and security.
     a.   Could you please describe the amount and kind of experience you have had in school safety?
     b.   To what extent has this experience pertained to the reporting of threats?

2.   BACKGROUND ON SCHOOL THREAT REPORTING SYSTEM
     a.   [DESCRIP] Can you provide a description of the threat reporting system(s) in place that your school/district uses?
          i.   How long has your system been in place?
          ii.   About how many reports do you receive per year?
          iii. [MODE] What types of reporting formats does your system make available to individuals reporting information? (e.g. phone, mobile app, web, multiple means)
          iv.   Is information provided anonymously? Confidentially? Some other way?
          v.   What features of this system or reporting process appeal most to your school/district's needs?
     b.   [TEAM] Can you provide a description of the district/school team(s) responsible for managing the system?
          i.   [REVIEW/PROCESS] Who fields reports and tips?
                •   *If state or other org fielding tips to school/district:* Can you describe your school/district's processes for fielding reports you received from *[state system name]*?
                •   What are your district/school protocols for working with law enforcement on responding to tips?
          ii.   Do any other stakeholders and community members play a role in the threat reporting process (e.g. students, parents, community health providers, etc.)?
     c.   [PROCESSING REPORTS] What happens to information received through the reporting system? [if using multiple systems- distinguish between state systems and non-state systems]

      i.   Where are threat reports forwarded? (e.g. school administrators, local police services, both, other entities?)

      ii.   Does the system have information sharing policies in place? With whom?

      iii. Is there a central district or school database through which reports/cases are tracked by the school/district? Who developed this? (e.g., district, school. . .)

      iv. What changes, if any, have you made to your district/school procedures? What prompted these changes?

      v.   What other information about the reporting system processes specific to your district/school do you think is important for districts/schools to consider?

  d.   [BUILDING AWARENESS] How do you build awareness of your reporting system and processes to staff, students, and families?

      i.   What training do team members processing reports receive?

      ii.   What guidance or training does the district/school provide to the reporting community (students, parents, staff)? [who created this/who delivers it]

         •   What's the focus of the guidance/training for these groups ?

      iii. How does your district/school share reporting information with your reporting community?

3.   PERCEPTIONS OF REPORTING EFFECTIVENESS

  a.   What key features or elements make reporting systems effective in school settings?

      i.   Probe if relevant: What about features specific to your district's/school's reporting processes, which do you find particularly effective?

  b.   Do you perceive that the threat reporting system(s) in place at your school/district/state is effective?

      i.   Why or why not? Can you provide examples of specific situations that you see as successes or missed opportunities?

  c.   Do you think that students and other community members view the reporting system as successful?

      i.   Why or why not? Can you provide some examples of situations that might support your response?

4.   APPROACHES TO ENCOURAGING REPORTING

  a.   What best practices and strategies have you identified in the design and implementation of school threat reporting systems/processes, particularly as this concerns building trust and encouraging students and others to come forward with information?

  b.   How does trust between law enforcement/school resource officers and students affect reporting?

  c.   What design features or implementation procedures do you think are uniquely important for school reporting systems?

5. BARRIERS TO REPORTING
    a. What barriers have you encountered in the implementation of threat reporting systems and/or district/school procedures, particularly as this relates to willingness to report threats?
        i. How have you or others addressed/overcome these barriers?
    b. What barriers do you see as unique to implementing threat reporting systems and processes in schools?
        i. How can schools/school districts address these barriers?

6. CONCLUDING QUESTIONS
    As we wrap up, we would now like to ask you:
    a. Is there anything else we did not cover that we should consider as we build our toolkit?
    b. Are there any other individuals or organizations you feel we should speak to who have good visibility on these issues and can provide valuable insight for our study? Can you provide their contact information?

Is there any additional documentation you could share with us that you think would be relevant?

Abbreviations

CSSRC   Colorado School Safety Resource Center
IP   internet protocol
K–12   kindergarten through 12th grade
LEA   local education agency
MDT   multidisciplinary team
NTAC   National Threat Assessment Center
SRO   school resource officer
TA   threat assessment
USSS   U.S. Secret Service

References

Aiello, Michael F., "Should I Call for Help? Examining the Influences of Situational Factors and Bystander Characteristics on Reporting Likelihood," *Journal of School Violence*, Vol. 18, No. 2, 2019, pp. 163–175.

Amman, Molly, Matthew Bowlin, Lesley Buckles, Kevin C. Burton, Kimberly F. Brunell, Karie A. Gibson, Sarah H. Griffin, Kirk Kennedy, and Cari J. Robins, *Making Prevention a Reality: Identifying, Assessing, and Managing the Threat of Targeted Attacks*, Washington, D.C.: Behavioral Analysis Unit, National Center for the Analysis of Violent Crime, Critical Incident Response Group, Federal Bureau of Investigation, U.S. Department of Justice, February 2017. As of June 9, 2022:
https://www.hsdl.org/?abstract&did=804728

Atkinson, Anne J., "Fostering School–Law Enforcement Partnerships," *Safe and Secure: Guides to Creating Safer Schools*, Guide 5, September 2002. As of June 9, 2022:
https://www.ojp.gov/ncjrs/virtual-library/abstracts/
fostering-school-law-enforcement-partnerships-guide-5-safe-and

Blad, Evie, "More Schools Are Using Anonymous Tip Lines to Thwart Violence. Do They Work?" *Education Week*, August 10, 2018.

Bolante, Rebecca, and Cass Dykeman, "Threat Assessment Teams for Institutions of Higher Education: A Review of Key Ideas and Practices for Professional Counselors," *VISTAS Online*, 2017, art. 29. As of June 14, 2022:
https://www.counseling.org/knowledge-center/vistas/by-subject2/vistas-crisis/docs/
default-source/vistas/Threat_Assessment_Teams#

Carlton, Mary Poulin, "School Safety: Research on Gathering Tips and Addressing Threats," *National Institute of Justice Journal*, Vol. 283, April 12, 2021. As of May 27, 2022:
https://nij.ojp.gov/topics/articles/school-safety-research-gathering-tips-and-addressing-threats

Center for Prevention Programs and Partnerships, U.S. Department of Homeland Security, "Threat Assessment and Management Teams," December 28, 2021. As of April 26, 2022:
https://www.dhs.gov/publication/threat-assessment-and-management-teams

CISA—*See* Cybersecurity and Infrastructure Security Agency.

Colorado Attorney General, *Safe2Tell Colorado 2018–2019 Annual Report*, 2019.

———, *Safe2Tell Annual Report*, 2020. As of May 5, 2022:
https://safe2tell.org/data/

Colorado School Safety Resource Center, Department of Public Safety, *Essentials of School Threat Assessment: Preventing Targeted School Violence*, updated April 2020. As of April 26, 2022:
https://cdpsdocs.state.co.us/safeschools/CSSRC%20Documents/
CSSRC_Essentials_of_TA_2020.pdf

Connell, Nadine M., Nina Barbieri, and Jennifer M. Reingle Gonzalez, "Understanding School Effects on Students' Willingness to Report Peer Weapon Carrying," *Youth Violence and Juvenile Justice*, Vol. 13, No. 3, July 2015, pp. 258–269.

Cornell, Dewey, "Threat Assessment in College Settings," *Change*, Vol. 42, No. 1, 2010, pp. 8–15.

———, "A Developmental Perspective on the Virginia Student Threat Assessment Guidelines," *New Directions for Youth Development*, Vol. 2011, No. 129, Spring 2011, pp. 43–59.

———, "Threat Assessment as a School Violence Prevention Strategy," *Criminology and Public Policy*, Vol. 19, No. 1, February 2020, pp. 235–252.

Cornell, Dewey, and Jennifer Maeng, *Student Threat Assessment as a Safe and Supportive Prevention Strategy: Final Technical Report*, Charlottesville, Va.: Curry School of Education, University of Virginia, February 2020. As of April 26, 2022:
https://nij.ojp.gov/library/publications/
student-threat-assessment-safe-and-supportive-prevention-strategy-final

Cornell, Dewey, Jennifer L. Maeng, Anna Grace Burnette, Yuane Jia, Francis Huang, Timothy Konold, Pooja Datta, Marisa Malone, and Patrick Meyer, "Student Threat Assessment as a Standard School Safety Practice: Results from a Statewide Implementation Study," *School Psychology Quarterly*, Vol. 33, No. 2, June 2018, pp. 213–222.

Craun, Sarah W., Karie A. Gibson, Amanda G. Ford, Kristen Solik, and James Silver, "(In)action: Variation in Bystander Responses Between Persons of Concern and Active Shooters," *Journal of Threat Assessment and Management*, Vol. 7, No. 1–2, 2020, pp. 113–121.

Crichlow-Ball, Caroline, and Dewey Cornell, "Association of School Climate with Student Willingness to Report Threats of Violence," *Journal of Threat Assessment and Management*, Vol. 8, No. 3, 2021, pp. 77–93.

CSSRC—*See* Colorado School Safety Resource Center.

Cybersecurity and Infrastructure Security Agency, "School Security Assessment Tool (SSAT)," webpage, undated. As of June 21, 2022:
https://www.cisa.gov/school-security-assessment-tool

———, *K–12 School Security Guide*, 3rd ed., 2022. As of June 21, 2022:
https://www.cisa.gov/k-12-school-security-guide

Doyle, Joanna, "Barriers and Facilitators of Multidisciplinary Team Working: A Review," *Paediatric Nursing*, Vol. 20, No. 2, March 2008, pp. 26–29.

Dwyer, Kevin, and David Osher, *Safeguarding Our Children: An Action Guide*, Washington, D.C.: U.S. Departments of Education and Justice and American Institutes for Research, 2000. As of April 26, 2022:
https://www2.ed.gov/admins/lead/safety/actguide/index.html

Eisenman, David P., and Louise Flavahan, "Canaries in the Coal Mine: Interpersonal Violence, Gang Violence, and Violent Extremism Through a Public Health Prevention Lens," *International Review of Psychiatry*, Vol. 29, No. 4, August 2017, pp. 341–349.

Eliot, Megan, Dewey Cornell, Anne Gregory, and Xitao Fan, "Supportive School Climate and Student Willingness to Seek Help for Bullying and Threats of Violence," *Journal of School Psychology*, Vol. 48, No. 6, December 2010, pp. 533–553.

Ellis, B. Heidi, and Saida Abdi, "Building Community Resilience to Violent Extremism Through Genuine Partnerships," *American Psychologist*, Vol. 72, No. 3, April 2017, pp. 289–300.

Ellis, B. Heidi, Alisa B. Miller, Ronald Schouten, Naima Y. Agalab, and Saida M. Abdi, "The Challenge and Promise of a Multidisciplinary Team Response to the Problem of Violent Radicalization," *Terrorism and Political Violence*, 2020, pp. 1–18.

Family Educational Rights and Privacy Act—*See* 20 U.S.C. § 1232g.

Fein, Robert A., Bryan Vossekuil, William S. Pollack, Randy Borum, William Modzeleski, and Marisa Reddy, *Threat Assessment in Schools: A Guide to Managing Threatening Situations and to Creating Safe School Climates*, Washington, D.C.: U.S. Secret Service and U.S. Department of Education, July 2004. As of June 15, 2022:
https://www2.ed.gov/admins/lead/safety/threatassessmentguide.pdf

FortifyFL, homepage, undated. As of April 26, 2022:
https://getfortifyfl.com/

Goodrum, Sarah, Andrew J. Thompson, Kyle C. Ward, and William Woodward, "A Case Study on Threat Assessment: Learning Critical Lessons to Prevent School Violence," *Journal of Threat Assessment and Management*, Vol. 5, No. 3, 2018, pp. 121–136.

Goodrum, Sarah, and William Woodward, *Report on the Arapahoe High School Shooting: Lessons Learned on Information Sharing, Threat Assessment, and Systems Integrity*, Denver: Denver Foundation and Colorado SB 15-214 Committee on School Safety and Youth in Crisis, January 18, 2016. As of April 26, 2022:
https://cspv.colorado.edu/wp-content/uploads/2019/03/
Report_on_the_Arapahoe_High_School_Shooting_FINAL.pdf

Gorman, Nicole, "Powerful PSA Encourages School Communities to See Something, Say Something to Prevent Violence," *Education World*, December 7, 2016. As of April 26, 2022:
https://www.educationworld.com/a_news/
powerful-psa-encourages-school-communities-see-something-say-something-prevent-violence

Haner, Murat, Melissa M. Sloan, Justin T. Pickett, and Francis T. Cullen, "When Do Americans 'See Something, Say Something'? Experimental Evidence on the Willingness to Report Terrorist Activity," *Justice Quarterly*, 2021, pp. 1–25.

Hansen, Rachel, and Melissa Diliberti, "What Are Threat Assessment Teams and How Prevalent Are They in Public Schools?" *NCES Blog*, July 10, 2018. As of April 26, 2022:
https://nces.ed.gov/blogs/nces/post/
what-are-threat-assessment-teams-and-how-prevalent-are-they-in-public-schools

Harrington, Lindsay S., "Civil/Student Tipster Immunity: Protecting Individuals Who Report Threats of Potential Violence from Defamation Liability," *McGeorge Law Review*, Vol. 33, No. 2, 2002, art. 3.

Henkel, Sarah J., *Threat Assessment Strategies to Mitigate Violence in Healthcare*, International Association for Healthcare Security and Safety, IAHSS-F RS-19-02, November 11, 2019. As of April 26, 2022:
https://iahssf.org/assets/
IAHSS-Foundation-Threat-Assessment-Strategies-to-Mitigate-Violence-in-Healthcare.pdf

Hodges, Heath J., Elizabeth C. Low, M. Rosa Viñas-Racionero, Brandon A. Hollister, and Mario J. Scalora, "Examining the Reasons for Student Responses to Threatening Behaviors on a College Campus," *Journal of Threat Assessment and Management*, Vol. 3, No. 3–4, 2016, pp. 129–142.

Hollister, Brandon, Mario Scalora, Sarah Hoff, and Alissa Marquez, "Exposure to Preincident Behavior and Reporting in College Students," *Journal of Threat Assessment and Management*, Vol. 1, No. 2, 2014, pp. 129–143.

Irwin, Katherine, Janet Davidson, and Amanda Hall-Sanchez, "The Race to Punish in American Schools: Class and Race Predictors of Punitive School-Crime Control," *Critical Criminology*, Vol. 21, No. 1, March 2013, pp. 47–71.

Johansson, Gudrun, Kajsa Eklund, and Gunilla Gosman-Hedström, "Multidisciplinary Team, Working with Elderly Persons Living in the Community: A Systematic Literature Review," *Scandinavian Journal of Occupational Therapy*, Vol. 17, No. 2, 2010, pp. 101–116.

Kelly, Shawna Rader, "The School Psychologist's Role in Leading Multidisciplinary School-Based Threat Assessment Teams," *Contemporary School Psychology*, Vol. 22, No. 2, June 2018, pp. 163–173.

Kenny, James, "Risk Assessment and Management Teams: A Comprehensive Approach to Early Intervention in Workplace Violence," *Journal of Applied Security Research*, Vol. 5, No. 2, 2010, pp. 159–175.

Kutash, Krista, Mary Acri, Michele Pollock, Kelsey Armusewicz, Su-chin Serene Olin, and Kimberly Eaton Hoagwood, "Quality Indicators for Multidisciplinary Team Functioning in Community-Based Children's Mental Health Services," *Administration and Policy in Mental Health and Mental Health Services Research*, Vol. 41, No. 1, January 2014, pp. 55–68.

Malone, Darren, Sarah V. L. Marriott, Giles Newton-Howes, Shaeda Simmonds, and Peter Tyrer, "Community Mental Health Teams (CMHTs) for People with Severe Mental Illnesses and Disordered Personality," *Cochrane Database of Systematic Reviews*, Vol. 2007, No. 3, July 2007, art. CD000270.

Maryland Center for School Safety, *Maryland's Model Policy for Behavior Threat Assessment*, September 2018. As of April 26, 2022:
https://schoolsafety.maryland.gov/Pages/RES-Reports-Data.aspx

———, *2020 Annual Report*, c. 2020. As of May 5, 2022:
https://schoolsafety.maryland.gov/Pages/RES-Reports-Data.aspx

Meckler, Laura, and Hannah Natanson, "How Can Schools Detect Potentially Violent Students? Researchers Have an Answer," *Washington Post*, December 9, 2021. As of April 26, 2022:
https://www.washingtonpost.com/education/2021/12/09/
stopping-school-mass-shootings-oxford-michigan/

Meloy, J. Reid, and Mary Ellen O'Toole, "The Concept of Leakage in Threat Assessment," *Behavioral Sciences and the Law*, Vol. 29, No. 4, July–August 2011, pp. 513–527.

Millspaugh Sara, Dewey Cornell, Pooja Datta, and Anna Heilbrun, Curry School of Education, University of Virginia, and Francis Huang, College of Education, University of Missouri, "Prevalence of Aggressive Attitudes and Student Willingness to Report Threats of Violence in Middle Schools," poster, Virginia Youth Violence Project, July 2015. As of April 26, 2022:
https://education.virginia.edu/sites/default/files/uploads/resourceLibrary/
FINAL_SaraM_PosterDraft_July7.pdf

Murphy, Kristina, and Julie Barkworth, "Victim Willingness to Report Crime to Police: Does Procedural Justice or Outcome Matter Most?" *Victims and Offenders*, Vol. 9, No. 2, 2014, pp. 178–204.

National Association of School Psychologists, "Threat Assessment at School," webpage, 2015. As of April 26, 2022:
https://www.nasponline.org/resources-and-publications/resources-and-podcasts/
school-safety-and-crisis/systems-level-prevention/threat-assessment-at-school

National Association of School Resource Officers, "Training Courses," webpage, undated. As of May 27, 2022:
https://www.nasro.org/training/training-courses/

National Association of SROs—*See* National Association of School Resource Officers.

National Threat Assessment Center, U.S. Secret Service, U.S. Department of Homeland Security, *Enhancing School Safety Using a Threat Assessment Model: An Operational Guide for Preventing Targeted School Violence*, Washington, D.C., July 2018. As of April 26, 2022:
https://www.cisa.gov/enhancing-school-safety-using-threat-assessment-model

———, *Averting Targeted School Violence: A U.S. Secret Service Analysis of Plots Against Schools*, Washington, D.C., March 2021. As of May 31, 2022:
https://www.secretservice.gov/protection/ntac

Nekvasil, Erin K., and Dewey G. Cornell, "Student Reports of Peer Threats of Violence: Prevalence and Outcomes," *Journal of School Violence*, Vol. 11, No. 4, 2012, pp. 357–375.

NTAC—*See* National Threat Assessment Center.

Office of Attorney General, Commonwealth of Pennsylvania, *Safe2Say Something Annual Report 2019–2020 School Year*, c. 2021. As of May 5, 2022:
https://www.safe2saypa.org/wp-content/uploads/2021/01/
2019-2020-S2SS-Annual-Report-FINAL.pdf

———, *Special Report on Student Mental Health*, c. 2022. As of May 27, 2022:
https://www.attorneygeneral.gov/wp-content/uploads/2022/04/
OAG_Special_Report_on_Student_Mental_Health.pdf

Office of Safe Schools, Florida Department of Education, *Model Behavioral Threat Assessment Policies and Best Practices for K–12 Schools*, May 2020. As of April 26, 2022:
https://www.fldoe.org/safe-schools/threat-assessment.stml

Okada, Dave, lieutenant, Salem (Oreg.) Police Department, "Community-Based Threat Assessment Teams: Partnerships for Safer Communities," briefing, Association of Threat Assessment Professionals Spring Regional Conference, 2015. As of April 26, 2022:
https://cdn.ymaws.com/www.atapworldwide.org/resource/resmgr/
Okada_-_Community_Based_Thre.pdf

Payne, Allison Ann, and Kelly Welch, "Restorative Justice in Schools: The Influence of Race on Restorative Discipline," *Youth and Society*, Vol. 47, No. 4, July 2015, pp. 539–564.

Payne, Susan R. T., and Delbert S. Elliott, "Safe2Tell®: An Anonymous, 24/7 Reporting System for Preventing School Violence," *New Directions for Youth Development*, Vol. 2011, No. 129, Spring 2011, pp. 103–111.

Planty, Michael, Duren Banks, Stacey Cutbush, and Jodi Sherwood, *School Tip Line Toolkit: A Blueprint for Implementation and Sustainability*, Research Triangle Park, N.C.: RTI International, 2018. As of April 26, 2022:
https://www.ojp.gov/pdffiles1/nij/grants/252537.pdf

Planty, Michael, Duren Banks, Christine Lindquist, Joel Cartwright, and Amanda Witwer, *Tip Lines for School Safety: A National Portrait of Tip Line Use*, Research Triangle Park, N.C.: RTI International, February 2020. As of April 26, 2022:
https://nij.ojp.gov/library/publications/tip-lines-school-safety-national-portrait-tip-line-use

Planty, Michael, Stacey Cutbush, Duren Banks, and D. D'Arcangelo, *School Safety Tip Line Toolkit*, Research Triangle Park, N.C.: RTI International, 2021. As of May 27, 2022:
https://www.rti.org/publication/school-safety-tip-line-toolkit/fulltext.pdf

Pollack, William S., William Modzeleski, and Georgeann Rooney, "Prior Knowledge of Potential School-Based Violence: Information Students Learn May Prevent a Targeted Attack," Washington, D.C.: U.S. Secret Service and U.S. Department of Education, May 2008. As of April 26, 2022:
https://eric.ed.gov/?id=ED511645

Public Law 107-296, Homeland Security Act of 2002, November 25, 2002. As of May 12, 2019:
https://www.govinfo.gov/app/details/PLAW-107publ296

Public Law 114-95, Every Student Succeeds Act, December 10, 2015. As of June 18, 2022:
https://www.govinfo.gov/app/details/PLAW-114publ95

Reeves, Melissa A. Louvar, and Stephen E. Brock, "School Behavioral Threat Assessment and Management," *Contemporary School Psychology*, Vol. 22, No. 2, June 2018, pp. 148–162.

Rengifo, Andres F., Lee Ann Slocum, and Vijay Chillar, "From Impressions to Intentions: Direct and Indirect Effects of Police Contact on Willingness to Report Crimes to Law Enforcement," *Journal of Research in Crime and Delinquency*, Vol. 56, No. 3, May 2019, pp. 412–450.

Rosand, E., "Multi-Disciplinary and Multi-Agency Approaches to Preventing and Countering Violent Extremism: An Emerging P/CVE Success Story?" *Global Terrorism Index 2018: Measuring the Impact of Terrorism*, Sydney, Australia: Institute for Economics and Peace, 2018.

Ryan-Arredondo, Kim, Kristin Renouf, Carla Egyad, Meridith Doxey, Maria Dobbins, Serafin Sanchez, and Bert Rakowitz, "Threats of Violence in Schools: The Dallas Independent School District's Response," *Psychology in the Schools*, Vol. 38, No. 2, March 2001, pp. 185–196.

Safe2Say Something, "Frequently Asked Questions," webpage, undated. As of May 27, 2022:
https://www.safe2saypa.org/faq/

Safe2Tell, "FAQ," webpage, undated a. As of May 27, 2022:
https://safe2tell.org/faq/

———, "History," webpage, undated b.

———, "Trainings and Presentations," webpage, undated c.

Saunders, Benjamin, Julius Sim, Tom Kingstone, Shula Baker, Jackie Waterfield, Bernadette Bartlam, Heather Burroughs, and Clare Jinks, "Saturation in Qualitative Research: Exploring Its Conceptualization and Operationalization," *Quality and Quantity*, Vol. 52, No. 4, July 2018, pp. 1893–1907. As of June 15, 2022:
https://link.springer.com/article/10.1007/s11135-017-0574-8

Schostak, Steven Benjamin, *Breaking Down Barriers to Reporting Threats of Targeted School Violence: Perceived Threat Seriousness as a Potential Mitigating Factor to the Student Bystander Effect*, dissertation, Fresno, Calif.: Alliant International University, Center for Forensic Studies, 2009. As of May 5, 2022:
https://www.proquest.com/docview/759979885?pq-origsite=gscholar&fromopenview=true

Seaman, Jessica, "What Colorado Can Learn from a Neighboring State's New Approach to Stopping Youth Suicide," *Loveland Reporter-Herald*, September 26, 2020. As of May 27, 2022:
https://www.reporterherald.com/2020/09/26/
police-response-teen-suicide-colorado-safe2tell-nebraska-safe2help/

Slocum, Lee Ann, Finn-Aage Esbensen, and Terrance J. Taylor, "The Code of Silence in Schools: An Assessment of a Socio-Ecological Model of Youth's Willingness to Report School Misbehavior," *Youth and Society*, Vol. 49, No. 2, March 2017, pp. 123–149.

Socia, Kelly M., Melissa S. Morabito, Brenda J. Bond, and Elias S. Nader, "Public Perceptions of Police Agency Fairness and the Willingness to Call Police," *American Review of Public Administration*, Vol. 51, No. 5, July 2021, pp. 360–373.

Stallings, Robert, and Jacob Christian Hall, "Averted Targeted School Killings from 1900–2016," *Criminal Justice Studies*, Vol. 32, No. 3, 2019, pp. 222–238.

Stein-Seroussi, Al, Sean Hanley, Marguerite Grabarek, and Tricia Woodliff, "Evaluating a Statewide Anonymous Reporting System for Students and Multidisciplinary Response Teams: Methods for a Randomized Trial," *International Journal of Educational Research*, Vol. 110, 2021, art. 101862.

Stohlman, Shelby L., and Dewey G. Cornell, "An Online Educational Program to Increase Student Understanding of Threat Assessment," *Journal of School Health*, Vol. 89, No. 11, November 2019, pp. 899–906.

Stone, Carolyn, and Madelyn L. Isaacs, "Involving Students in Violence Prevention: Anonymous Reporting and the Need to Promote and Protect Confidences," *NASSP Bulletin*, Vol. 86, No. 633, December 2002, pp. 54–65.

Stueve, Ann, Kimberly Dash, Lydia O'Donnell, Parisa Tehranifar, Renée Wilson-Simmons, Ronald G. Slaby, and Bruce G. Link, "Rethinking the Bystander Role in School Violence Prevention," *Health Promotion Practice*, Vol. 7, No. 1, January 2006, pp. 117–124.

Sulkowski, Michael L., "An Investigation of Students' Willingness to Report Threats of Violence in Campus Communities," *Psychology of Violence*, Vol. 1, No. 1, 2011, pp. 53–65.

Syvertsen, Amy K., Constance A. Flanagan, and Michael D. Stout, "Code of Silence: Students' Perceptions of School Climate and Willingness to Intervene in a Peer's Dangerous Plan," *Journal of Educational Psychology*, Vol. 101, No. 1, 2009, pp. 219–232.

Unnever, James D., and Dewey G. Cornell, "Middle School Victims of Bullying: Who Reports Being Bullied?" *Aggressive Behavior*, Vol. 30, No. 5, 2004, pp. 373–388.

U.S. Code, Title 6, Domestic Security; Chapter 1, Homeland Security Organization; Subchapter III, Science and Technology in Support of Homeland Security; Section 185, Federally Funded Research and Development Centers. As of March 20, 2021: https://uscode.house.gov/view.xhtml?req=(title:6%20section:185%20edition:prelim)

———, Title 20, Education; Chapter 31, General Provisions Concerning Education; Subchapter III, General Requirements and Conditions Concerning Operation and Administration of Education Programs: General Authority of Secretary; Part 4, Records; Privacy; Limitation on Withholding Federal Funds; Section 1232g, Family Educational and Privacy Rights. As of June 17, 2022: https://uscode.house.gov/view.xhtml?req=(title:20%20section:1232g%20edition:prelim)

Virginia Center for School and Campus Safety, Virginia Department of Criminal Justice Services, *Threat Assessment and Management in Virginia Public Schools: Model Policies, Procedures, and Guidelines*, revised July 2020. As of April 26, 2022: https://www.dcjs.virginia.gov/sites/dcjs.virginia.gov/files/publications/law-enforcement/threat-assessment-model-policies-procedures-and-guidelinespdf_0.pdf

Vossekuil, Bryan, Robert A. Fein, Marisa Reddy, Randy Borum, and William Modzeleski, *The Final Report and Findings of the Safe School Initiative: Implications for the Prevention of School Attacks in the United States*, Washington, D.C.: U.S. Department of Education, Office of Elementary and Secondary Education, Safe and Drug-Free Schools Program, and U.S. Secret Service National Threat Assessment Center, 2004. As of April 26, 2022: https://www2.ed.gov/admins/lead/safety/preventingattacksreport.pdf

Weine, Stevan, David P. Eisenman, La Tina Jackson, Janni Kinsler, and Chloe Polutnik, "Utilizing Mental Health Professionals to Help Prevent the Next Attacks," *International Review of Psychiatry*, Vol. 29, No. 4, August 2017, pp. 334–340.

Weine, Stevan, M. Masters, and L. Tartaglia, *Targeted Violence Intervention Best Practice Summit: After Action Report*, unpublished report of the Targeted Violence Intervention Best Practice Summit, Chicago, Ill., 2015.

Woitaszewski, Scott, Franci Crepeau-Hobson, Christina Conolly, and Melinda Cruz, "Rules, Requirements, and Resources for School-Based Threat Assessment: A Fifty State Analysis," *Contemporary School Psychology*, Vol. 22, June 2018, pp. 125–134.

Wylie, Lindsey E., Chris L. Gibson, Eve M. Brank, Mark R. Fondacaro, Stephen W. Smith, Veda E. Brown, and Scott A. Miller, "Assessing School and Student Predictors of Weapons Reporting," *Youth Violence and Juvenile Justice*, Vol. 8, No. 4, October 2010, pp. 351–372.

Yablon, Yaacov B., "Student–Teacher Relationships and Students' Willingness to Seek Help for School Violence," *Journal of Social and Personal Relationships*, Vol. 27, No. 8, December 2010, pp. 1110–1123.

———, "Combining Teaching and Counseling Roles: Implications for Students' Willingness to Seek Help for Bullying," *International Journal for the Advancement of Counselling*, Vol. 42, December 2020, pp. 382–392.